Walking Victims:

*Understanding and Treating
Abused Women Who
Repeat the Cycle*

Adele Mayer, Ph.D.

L𝐏 LEARNING PUBLICATIONS, INC.
Holmes Beach, Florida

ISBN 1-55691-126-2

Learning Publications, Inc.
5351 Gulf Drive
P.O. Box 1338
Holmes Beach, FL 34218-1338

Printing: 5 4 3 2 1   Year: 10 9 8 7

Printed in the United States of America.

Contents

Introduction v

Part One:
Overview of Target Population

1: Dysfunctional Abusive Families 3

Part Two:
Types of Abused Women

2: Survivors of Misfortune 9

Case Example • Therapy with Survivors of Misfortune • Treatment Goals

3: Unintentional Game Players or Adult Children of Double-Bind Parents 17

Case Example • Traits of Borderline Personalities • Therapy for Victims of Double-Bind Parenting • Specific Goals to Provide Information • Information for Clients on Double-Bind Parenting • Effects on the Child Who Has Had Double-Bind Parents • Information for Clients on Defenses • Traits of Potential Abusers

4: Intentional Game Players: Women with Unresolved Victim Bonding 33

Case Example • Psychopathic Maneuver • Case Example • Traits of Antisocial Personalities • Therapy for Victims with Unresolved Victim Bonds • Written Exercises

5: True Victims: Women with Histories of
   Early Unresolved Trauma 47

Case Example • Traits of Women Severely Abused as
Children • Therapy for Victims with Histories of Severe,
Unresolved Abuse • Social Casework Services for Victims of
Severe Abuse • Goals for Time-Limited Psychotherapy with
Victim's of Severe Abuse

Part 3:
Special Considerations

6: General Concerns with Abused Women 63

Externalization or Other Orientedness • Anger • Case
Example • Attachment • Traumatic Bonding • Traumatic
Bond • Learned Helplessness and Battered Women's
Syndrome • The Cycle of Abuse • Addiction • Addictive
Relationships

7: A Word about the Abuser 85

Traits of Batterers

8: Conclusion: Healthy, Survivor, or Victim?....91

Appendix A: Continuum of Abuse by Types 95

Appendix B: Childhood Imprints 99

Appendix C: Additional Exercises for Adult
Battered Women 103

Appendix D: Survey of Battered Women 119

Annotated Reading List 127

References 131

Introduction

The facts reveal the monumental challenge to counselors, therapists, psychologists, social workers, physicians, attorneys, and those working to improve societal conditions for women abuse survivors. Every 15 seconds, a woman in the United States is battered by her partner. Four women die daily at the hands of abusers (Hawker and Bicehouse 1995). Each year, 2.5 million cases of battering are reported (Dutton 1995). Domestic violence is the leading cause of injury to women in the United States (Jones 1994).

Domestic violence victims come from various socioeconomic, ethnic, and racial backgrounds and the range of abuse runs the gamut from critical rejection and scapegoating to murder.

The recent O.J. Simpson murder trial has spurred tremendous interest in and concern for the plight of women abused by their partners. Much of the attention has rightly focused on the serious issues of institutionalized behavior supporting hostile attitudes toward women and the need to hold men accountable for their brutality. The problem, involving 20 to 50 percent of couples in the United States, should arouse public outrage (NIMH pamphlet 1995).

The literature on domestic violence, often redundant, traditionally supports the theories of learned helplessness, the cycle of violence and inter-mittent reinforcement (learning theory) intensifying learned helplessness, and the effects of post-trau-matic stress. For example, Walker (1990) reports in her studies that the cycle of violence, with its ordi-nary complimentary relationship to learned helpless-ness, occurred in two-thirds of 1,600 incidents. The male has power, and he begins and ends the cycle.

Angry, chemical-abusing, dependent men — with control and power needs — find partners who are also dependent with low self-esteem. Learned helplessness and immobility are thought to be re-sponsible for inaction by these women who are paralyzed to take positive steps on behalf of them-selves and their children. And, since the batterer's behavior is random and unpredictable, intermittent reinforcement (the most difficult learned behavior to extinguish) exacerbates the woman's passivity. In-variably, she is diagnosed as experiencing the Bat-tered Woman's Syndrome, a category of Post-Traumatic Stress Disorder, with impairments in the behavioral, cognitive, and affective spheres.

Usually, the proposed solution is for the couple to separate. The male might be court-ordered into anger-management classes or incarcerated, and the female, referred to therapy with an orientation to-ward personal growth, economic self-sufficiency, and enhanced self-worth.

The recovery movement and women's aware-ness groups have promoted the stereotypic perception of a "jock" culture, i.e., "boys will be boys," by supporting the image of powerless female victims who bear no responsibility for abusive adult relationships. Feminists advocate an over-generalized historical/political perspective on battering and reject individual variables and psychological approaches.

Women's groups focus on the need to change the laws and societal attitudes that promote male dominance. But while legal and cultural improvements are needed, these groups indict mental health professionals, referring to pernicious psychiatric victim-blaming by mislabeling the effects of post traumatic stress for personality disorders; describing battered women as masochistic, provocative, and hysterical; focusing on why victims remain in abusive relationships rather than why abusers choose to batter (Jones 1994); and stigmatizing victims as codependent and addictive.

Feminists are correct in regarding battering as a crime rather than as a marital issue. However, discounting psychological factors is as biased as refusing to consider social, historical, and economic variables. Battering is an interactive problem involving two individuals with interpersonal dynamics related to their past histories. To question and seek an understanding of underlying dynamics is not to judge or blame. Even Gelles and Straus (1988) question whether violence precedes the problems or whether the problems produce the stress that leads to violence.

It is interesting that denial of the female role in spousal abuse prevails when the literature on relationships in general supports the concept of equal responsibility for the dynamics involved. Dutton, an expert on spousal abusers, clearly states that there is no "deficit" in the personality of a battered woman who is "trapped" in the relationship (1995).

Examination of the female's active role in the battering relationship in no way negates the validity of male accountability for actual battery that results from the underlying dynamics. The essential point is that focusing solely on altering male thinking and behavior patterns will not alleviate the problem of abusive relationships. Females play a vital role in the twisted interplay resulting in domestic violence. Because of the female role, countless numbers of women continue to return to their abusive partners (or find new abusers) once they have left the home and received needed support and guidance.

Many victims, regardless of their demographic and ethnic backgrounds, have been abused as children — sexually, and often physically and psychologically as well (Jones 1994). They share the same borderline, traumatic bonding and attachment issues as their tormentors. It is these women who are the focus of this book.

The goal is to provide a tentative typology of females in terms of the particular types of abuse they experienced as children and the resultant symptomatology. Realistic management and treatment strategies are then suggested. The categories proposed are not rigid: there may be considerable overlap, which is expected in view of the similarities in the backgrounds of these adult women.

Imprints left by the histories of victimized women result in vulnerability to abuse. However, depending upon the nature of the particular abuse experienced, adult victims do vary in their pathology with symptoms, including:

■ confusion regarding what is normal and abnormal;

■ a tendency to relive childhood abuse through adult relationships;

■ a quest for victim bonding;

■ an avenue to vent hostility through what many of these women call "the game";

■ flirtation with violence resulting from crisis-prone personalities.

It is the intention of this book that a deeper approach to specific subgroups of abused women will:

- generate interest and research into more effective treatment approaches, and

- lead to a closer examination of simplistic formulae involving gender responsibility in abusive relationships.

Part One:
Overview of Target Population

1
Dysfunctional Abusive Families

Since this book focuses on women who were sexually, or physically, and psychologically abused as children, it is appropriate to provide a brief, descriptive overview of their dysfunctional families of origin. It is these families that have left the strong imprints resulting in adult victimization.

Dysfunctional families share certain characteristics. They lack honesty, empathy, and genuine concern for others. Communication is poor and often indirect, with family members motivated by hidden agendas. In order to maintain the status quo, these families avoid noncoercive therapy because treatment would disrupt comfortable patterns, generate change, and possibly heighten already-existing fears of abandonment.

Enmeshment and interdependence characterize the dysfunctional family. Children are symbiotically connected to the parents and maintain the illusion that the mother and father are okay, while they, the children, are not okay. Punishments are random, unpredictable and severe, often dependent on the parents' erratic moods and inability to tolerate stress. Molestation is common, inter- and intragenerational, and unusually involves male perpetrators, including fathers, stepfathers, brothers, grandfathers, and uncles.

Because of the strong fear of abandonment in these families, psychological growth is discouraged. If any members gain insights that might lead to positive behavioral changes, they face scapegoating and psychological abuse until the status quo is reinstated. Conflicts remain hidden and unresolved.

These families tend to stereotype and label others with rigid, traditional thinking. Differences are discouraged because autonomy and independence threaten the integrity of the family unit. Boundaries are blurred with children often scapegoated to divert the focus away from family problems and to enhance denial.

Pathology is manifested by continual crises (jobs, illnesses, evictions, and so forth) which further bond family members, chemical abuse by parents and adolescents, delinquent behavior by minor children, domestic violence, and physical and sexual abuse of the children.

Often the families are involved with behavioral health systems with frequent psychiatric hospitalizations for parents or children, hospitalizations for psychogenic problems, financial state subsidies and food stamps, involvement with the courts for violence and abuse, investigations by protective services, and referrals to juvenile courts for the children's delinquency.

The children in these families often appear to be pseudo-mature, as they assume the roles of caretakers and protectors for one or both parents. This is especially common in incestuous families in which the enmeshed triad includes the victim, offender, and silent partner. The victim keeps the family secret in order to satisfy the needs of the father while protecting the mother from direct knowledge of the abuse.

Children in dysfunctional families often have attachment disorders with disruptions in developmental stages. Mistreated and objectified often since infancy, they are untrusting, ambivalent, frightened and insecure and have learned that love is conditional, attainable through manipulation and deception.

These children have experienced interruptions in developmental stages and, later in life, suffer from regression with inordinate primal need fulfillment. Symbiotically bonded to parents who have inhibited growth and autonomy, they remain emotional infants with poor coping and social skills, inability to function independently, lacking in judgment, and impulsive with low frustration tolerance. They suffer from identity confusion, blurred boundaries, lack of core identity, low self-worth, and they tend to repeat victim-perpetrator-rescuer roles throughout their lives.

Shamed and feeling responsible for the abuse experienced, they dissociate and block memories of traumatic events. Denial, minimization and rationalization are common defenses used to protect the fragile self from reality. Illusions and fantasies are pervasive and the belief system is distorted to enable acceptance of dysfunctional patterns in their families. These victims function through manipulation and continuation of the victim-rescuer-perpetrator roles.

In general, these children suffer from post-traumatic stress with impairments in emotional, cognitive, and behavioral areas. They are chronically depressed with underlying anger (either inhibited or excessive) with self-destructive or acting-out behaviors. As adults, they bear the labels of borderline or antisocial personalities.

Therapy is difficult with dysfunctional families because of resistance both to change and to interventions into unhealthy family alliances. Accepted treatment approaches rely on Reality, Behavioral and Cognitive Therapy, Environmental Manipulation, and Stress Management. Because these families manipulate and tend to pit therapists against one another, it helps to identify goals clearly; use behavioral, time-limited contracts; deal with issues sequentially; provide homework assignments; and closely monitor progress.

Part Two:
Types of Abused Women

2
Survivors
of Misfortune

There is no set profile describing abusers, who, despite high-risk indicators, may be hard to identify. Therefore, some survivors of childhood abuse marry these men simply because they are so numerous in the general population. In these cases, there are no hidden agendas, no secondary gains, and no manipulation or games. Sometimes, the relationships last for years, especially those involving emotional abuse, because of:

■ religious prohibitions on divorce,

■ economic considerations,

■ the slow progression of the abuse that results in victim rationalization and minimization,

■ consideration of children's needs,

- lack of awareness due to the insidiousness of the abuse,

- lack of extended family support,

- a culture that condones violence,

- misperceptions regarding the normality of male aggression.

It is not uncommon for female victims to begin to examine their relationships with their spouses when the children are ready to leave home. Or perhaps the women have advanced sufficiently in their careers to feel increased self-worth and economic independence.

Often, when these women do begin to assert and liberate themselves, the floodgates open. They realize how controlled and belittled they have been, and tremendous anger surfaces. They are unable to reverse their course of action even though their spouses may feel remorseful, frightened about losing their families, and committed to change.

The irony in these marriages is that anger and resolve strengthen the women who fare well emotionally, financially, and socially, following divorce. By contrast, their spouses, emotionally stuck at the tyrannical toddler stage of development, are very frightened about feelings of abandonment and having to face the likelihood they will have to become self-sufficient without convenient scapegoats on whom to displace anger and project responsibility for their failings.

If the children from these marriages are adolescents or older, they usually understand the dynamics of their parents' relationships very well, feeling either pride or resentment toward their mothers' new-found assertiveness, along with a sense of responsibility to take care of Dad. These children are confused, especially as the established roles of controlling father and dominated mother begin to shift.

Case Example

Karen, mother of four teenaged children, had been married to Bob for over 19 years. On the surface, the couple appeared to be compatible, with shared interests and a similar philosophy of child-rearing.

As a child, Karen had been sexually victimized by her maternal uncle. When the abuse was disclosed, Karen's parents were supportive and believed her. There was no further contact with the perpetrator although criminal action was not pursued.

Early in the marriage, when Karen avoided sexual intimacy with Bob, the couple sought marital counseling for about three months. Their sexual relationship improved as they implemented relaxation techniques, learned more effective communication, and began to understand the dynamics and effects of molestation.

When Karen reached the age of 40, she went to a therapist to determine if she were "crazy." She said that her life looked perfect from the outside, that all of her friends envied her, and that she did not understand why she felt miserable most of the time.

As Karen spoke, she described a marriage in which Bob was the controller. He made the decisions for her, the children, and himself. Bob also managed all of the family's finances, even though Karen had returned to work five years earlier and, as an executive secretary, could have been financially self-sufficient.

Bob belittled and criticized Karen's decisions about everything, including her decisions about the home decor, discipline of the children, housekeeping, wardrobe, and work hours. He wanted her to work outside of the home for additional income but resented her time away from him. He felt she neglected her housekeeping duties and did not cook often enough for the family.

When the couple fought, Bob often referred to her "crazy incest family" to explain her incompetence. He used her background to further diminish her self-esteem and to try to make her feel that only he could love a woman with such a damaged past.

For the past four years, Bob had become very demanding sexually. When Karen balked about having sexual intercourse 10 to 15 times per week, Bob told her she needed therapy to resolve her childhood hang-ups. He called her "frigid," "cold," and "uncaring." There were a number of times when Karen would awaken in the middle of the night to find Bob on top of her forcing oral sex.

Bob also controlled the children, especially as they reached adolescence and wanted some degree of autonomy. He insisted on knowing where they were at all times and grounded them for days at a time for minor infractions. When the teenagers returned from dates, Bob smelled their breaths to detect any signs of drinking, and interrogated them about the details of their activities. Karen and the children resented Bob's intrusiveness and constant interference, especially since the teenagers did not have any obvious emotional or behavioral problems.

At the end of three treatment sessions, Karen told her therapist that she had decided to seek divorce. The therapist asked, "Is that why you originally came . . . for permission to divorce?" Karen thought for a moment and replied, "I think so."

Therapy with Survivors of Misfortune

Unless there is some deeper pathology, treatment with these survivors generally is short-term with an excellent prognosis. Often the children require treatment because of their empathy for their father and tendency to become caretakers. There also may be resentment against the mother for dissolving the family unit along with an awareness and understanding about her reasons for doing so.

Treatment Goals

1) These women need validation for the often subtle, yet corrosive abuse they have experienced over the years. A Rogerian approach involving active listening and attending behaviors, unconditional acceptance, reflection, and clarification is suggested to enable the women to sort through their feelings, clarify values and goals, understand the nature of abusive relationships, and make healthy choices regarding the future.

2) If victims request marital counseling, it is important that they maintain their new assertiveness to avoid any manipulation by their spouses. The prospect of impending divorce sometimes causes sufficient pain and suffering to motivate an offending spouse to effect needed change, at least temporarily. Therapy should be time limited with measurable goals and objectives as well as contracts to ensure adherence to goals. Contingencies for noncompliance should be established, including the possibility of legal separation.

3) Family sessions with the mother and children are helpful if divorce is imminent to allow for

ventilation, improve communication, clarify roles, and establish that neither the children, nor the mother, is responsible for Dad.

4) Family sessions with both parents are indicated if the couple decides to work through their problems as a unit. The children need to express concerns and feelings about the family with the parents setting appropriate limits about issues that involve all family members and those that involve the adults only.

3
Unintentional Game Players or Adult Children of Double-Bind Parents

Double-bind parenting, in the extreme, can result in serious mental incapacitation.* Generally, this style of child-rearing leads to offspring with trust issues, confusion regarding what is normal and what is not, and abandonment issues.

Double-bind parents are characterized by giving mixed messages to their children. An employed, overstressed mother with an active social life tells her children, whom she rarely sees, how much they mean to her. Another mother ignores molestation perpetrated upon her daughters by their older brothers.

---

*Often, these women have developed borderline personalities.

A father might be loving one moment and sexually abusive the next, or he might scream at the children with no apparent provocation other than his own low-tolerance threshold. A parent, when calm, tells his child how intelligent she is; then, in anger, yells, "You stupid slut!" Another parent might verbally ask for hugs while nonverbally conveying the message that the child should distance herself. These scenarios are emotionally abusive to a child who receives mixed, confusing messages about her self-worth and parents' inconsistency and instability.

The adult child of double-bind parents inherits a legacy of confusion, of polarizing relationships, and approaching life as black and white. This rigidity provides her with a defense against an unpredictable world which randomly treats her well or abusively, regardless of how she, herself, acts. Therefore, this adult is vulnerable to abuse since she lacks any measure of normalcy with which to gage her own behaviors or assess the behaviors of others. Either she trusts too easily or not at all, based solely on the emotional reactions of others.

Boundaries, sometimes with the same individual, are either too rigid or too flexible. She craves intimacy and closeness yet may distance herself before experiencing expected rejection. Abandonment is feared, yet anticipated and even desired, since relationships are perceived as conflicted, painful, and only occasionally gratifying. Relationships are also seen as either good or bad with few gray areas because it is easier to categorize than discriminate when there has been a history of poor role modeling to teach discrimination.

For this woman, life is generally unsatisfying, with a reliance on fantasies and illusions to compensate for painful reality. In sum, this adult child is vulnerable to abuse because she lives in a perpetual state of limbo, buffeted by confusing messages from childhood and lacking coping strategies to function successfully in the adult world. In a futile quest to manipulate successfully her environment and relationships, she becomes an unintentional game player, lacking authenticity and guided only by the emotions of the moment.

The woman is a true co-dependent, enmeshed with significant others, a people-pleaser and caretaker with a strong need to be needed. She is obsessed with changing and controlling the behavior of significant others and seeks partners to rescue, mold, and fix. Ultimately, she holds the power in her relationships.

Case Example

Kelly, aged 21, is an example of the adult child of double-bind parents. As a child, she felt closer to Dad, who was warm and loving, while Mom was perceived as emotionally distant and indifferent. Kelly described herself as a "daddy's girl" and was a constant companion on his out-of-state sales trips.

Kelly's father molested her for six years start-
ing on her fifth birthday. The abuse was physically
gentle with Dad always asking permission to touch
or be touched. He also gratified her material wishes
and turned to her both to give and ask for comfort
and nurturing.

The messages Kelly received from her father
were that loving, caring people do bad things, love
is conditional, and rewards come with performance.
Kelly's confusion was further compounded when
she began to mature and develop physically. At that
time, her father suddenly stopped molesting her. Instead, he became verbally abusive, called her a
"slut" and a "whore," and closely monitored her
behavior with boys. At 14, when she had a steady
boyfriend, Dad said: "Remember, you can't do anything with him that you wouldn't do with me."

Throughout her childhood, Kelly's mother
maintained emotional distance. Kelly later described
her mother as "someone who probably knew about
the abuse and was jealous of my relationship with
Dad." From her mother, Kelly received the messages that people who are expected to care for you
cannot be trusted; you cannot expect protection; and
blurred roles and boundaries are the norm.

Kelly wanted to please both parents, to comply
with Dad's demands to meet his needs while protecting Mom from open recognition of the family
secrets. She emerged from this abusive, double-bind

background confused and wanting to please, yet fearful of rejection.

Kelly felt responsible for her relationships; did not know how a normal family operated; had no conception of what constituted appropriated roles and boundaries; and behaved as though trust were inconstant, unreliable and variable, dependent not on predictability but fluctuating with the reactions of the moment. Her mode of operating in the world was reactive rather than proactive.

Kelly's first long-term relationship at age 18 involved a man 12 years her senior. He made sexual demands on her, coercing her to engage in anal intercourse and submit to vaginal sex two to three times daily. She complied with his every demand while hoping (and fully expecting) that he would change with the recognition that he truly loved her. It was he who broke off the relationship when he tired of her.

Subsequent boyfriends beat, raped, and emotionally abused Kelly. One characteristic these men shared in common was a "loving nature" combined with abusive behaviors. In these relationships, Kelly played the same role of caretaker and pleaser, rationalizing that her lovers would change, and minimizing the abuse she experienced.

By age 29, Kelly felt "stuck" — alone and unfulfilled. To protect her low self-image, she rationalized her past relationships, blamed herself for not

trying harder to please her partners, and idealized
the men with whom she had been involved. "If only
. . ." was the theme by which she lived. She fully
trusted her boyfriends, renounced her values and
fragile sense of self to meet their needs, craved intimacy, and blamed herself for her emotional distanc-
ing which she believed resulted in the dissolution of
her relationships.

Traits of Borderline Personalities

■ Severe abandonment issues — fears abandonment and rejection; distances self from others to
avoid abandonment; has approach-avoidance
style of relating.

■ Identity issues — lacks a core sense of identity;
manifests chameleon-like behaviors and poor
boundaries.

■ Emptiness — is bored easily; needs change and
variety to fill inner void; catastrophizes and is
crisis prone.

■ Self-destruction — is prone to suicidal threats,
gestures and attempts; self-mutilates, often has
eating disorders.

■ Inappropriate expression of anger — severely
overreacts, often explosively.

■ Mood shifts — has unpredictable changes in
moods, often with no easily identified triggers.

■ Impulsivity — acts without forethought; exercises poor judgment.

■ Antisocial behaviors — acts out sexually; abuses chemicals; shoplifts; drives recklessly.

■ Variable relationships — has unstable and intense relationships with splitting the same person into "good" or "bad;" alternately devalues and idealizes; projects; and bases evaluations of others on most recent encounter.

Therapy for Victims of Double-Bind Parenting

Victims of double-bind parenting are confused and do not understand appropriate roles or what constitutes normal versus abnormal relationships. As with all clients, treatment needs should be individualized and tailored to meet the specific concerns of each woman. However, a necessary component of therapy with these victims is cognitive-educational information. The client should be assured that change is possible once problem areas are identified.

Specific Goals to Provide Information

Double-bind parenting and its effects, particularly confusion, insecurity, and problems with abandonment.

Information for Clients on Double-Bind Parenting

Explanation: Parents give mixed, confusing messages such as a loving father who molests his daughter; or a mother who professes devotion to her children, but is never available to them.

Effects on the Child Who Has Had Double-Bind Parents

- Feels insecure and confused; is never certain of how to interpret parental messages; lacks a sense of internal and external stability.

- Devalues her own worth from the negative impact of parental messages such as, "I love you as a father and I want to have sex with you."

- Sees relationships as conditional on certain behaviors but is unable to decipher what behaviors are expected in order to feel accepted.

- Trusts either too easily or not at all since parents were never able to model appropriate foundation for trust.

- Compartmentalizes following duality of relationships in family of origin; generalizes from the particular but does so inappropriately. For example, a child needs and wants a good father; her father is loving despite molestation; the child then labels Dad as a good father, ignoring or blocking the negative impact of abuse.

- Lives with fantasies, illusions, and potentials rather than reality, in part because of confusion as to what constitutes reality, and in part because fantasy is a balm for the pain of conflicted relationships.

- Has problems with boundaries that are either too flexible or too inflexible. The victim desires to merge with her partner and may be clinging and demanding; on the other hand, she fears engulfment or rejection and may distance herself. This results in unintentional game playing that confuses her partners and may incite their rage.

- Fears and, at the same time, hopes for abandonment; manifests a push-pull or approach-avoidance dynamic in relationships. The victim wants intimacy but has an underlying fear of rejection and manipulation. In anticipation of rejection, she withdraws or alienates herself from significant others, again setting the stage for frustration and potential abuse by her partner.

Defenses and their inappropriate use, consciously or unconsciously, resulting in dysfunctional relationships.

Information for Clients on Defenses

Explanation: In general, defenses are normal
and self-protective. Defenses become problematic
when they operate inappropriately and primitively
to enable dysfunctional reactions and behaviors. For
example, it is appropriate for a three-year-old boy to
deny that Dad is bigger and stronger than he is. It is
not appropriate for an adult victim to deny that her
perpetrator-father molested her as a child.

There are several defenses commonly used by
abused women (consciously or unconsciously)

- Denial — Denial works on a continuum with
  rationalization and minimization. People
  consciously or unconsciously use denial to
  maintain positive feelings about their behavior or the behavior of other individuals. In
  some instances, denial can be healthy when
  individuals need protection from being over-
  whelmed by reality. For example, terminally
  ill patients deny their prognoses initially. For
  these individuals, reality may be too painful
  to absorb.

Usually, however, denial should be worked
through in order to reach an acceptance of reality so
that healthy coping strategies may be implemented.
A mother of an incest victim may at first deny that
her husband is a perpetrator, but it is essential for

her to confront that denial, support her child, and accept the reality of abuse.

Because denial enables them to continue in
their relationships, emotionally and physically
abused women deny, rationalize, and minimize perpetrators' behaviors. For these women, this use of
denial in any of its forms is unhealthy, nonfunctional, and potentially lethal.

- Intellectualization — Intellectualizing behaviors preclude consideration of feelings. A
  woman who is angry at her abusive spouse
  and wants to leave him may have ambiva-
  lence due to underlying fear of independence
  or financial hardship. Her conflict creates a
  state of disequilibrium or cognitive disso-
  nance mandating resolution. One way to
  reach resolution is through splitting, e.g., intellectualizing and rationalizing while discounting the feelings involved. She may say
  her spouse is a good father and provider, and
  does not want to hurt anyone. Or, the victim
  tells herself she loves her partner and he
  loves her, while discounting the fact that he
  abuses her.

- Projection — Projection involves attributing
  one's feelings to another person. A victim,
  emotionally hurt by years of abuse, both as a
  child and adult, describes her partner as hurt
  because of events that occurred during his

own formative years. Her perception may or
may not coincide with reality, but it helps
her to rationalize remaining in an unhealthy
relationship. In reality, her spouse may be a
sadist who is detached from feelings. By attributing her own feelings to her partner, the
adult victim allows herself to understand,
empathize, minimize, and ultimately accept
his abuse. It also allows her covertly to give
him permission to abdicate responsibility for
the choices he makes as an adult.

• Displacement — Displacement often operates early in an abusive relationship. An
adult victimized by her father's molestation
or physical abuse has never resolved early
childhood trauma. Anger has been suppressed until she chooses a partner with
traits similar to those of her father. Anger
that should have been directed toward her father is displaced onto her partner. He, in
turn, becomes frustrated and angry. In time,
without understanding or resolution of underlying trauma, rage in the relationship may
escalate to violent behavior.

**Elements of a Healthy Functional Relation-
ship Versus Nonfunctional Relationships.** Because of poor role modeling, victims of double-bind
parents are not able to differentiate between normal
and abnormal relationships. They need to be educated regarding mature functional partnerships.

Healthy Relationships	Unhealthy Relationships
• clear boundaries with partner	• blurred or absent boundaries with partner
• mutual respect	• lack of self-respect and respect for partner
• trust between partners	• absence of trust between partners
• open, honest communication between partners	• serious problems with communication between partners
• strong sense of self for both partners	• weak sense of self for both partners
• awareness of needs and and feelings of self and partner	• marginal or absent awareness of needs and feelings of self and partner
• independent and goal-orientedness yet concerned about goals and interests of partner	• dependence and enmeshment with focus solely on relationship
• ability to feel and demonstrate love and caring	• concern with how partner makes her feel; unable to love
• interests in common with partner; some interests independent of partner's	• interests secondary to feelings and needs
• choices made in accordance with values and goals	• choices made on basis of feelings and needs of the moment
• ability to integrate thoughts and feelings	• separation of thoughts and feelings
• positive self-image	• devaluation of self
• nonexploitative sexual relationship based on mutual needs and wants	• sexual relationship based on selfishness and need fulfillment

High-risk indicators for potential abusers. It is not possible to predict which individuals will become abusive. However, there is a cluster of traits or characteristics associated with abusers.

Traits of Potential Abusers

■ abuses or has abused drugs and alcohol

■ has a history of violent behavior or violence in family of origin

■ has a history of emotional problems or mental illness

■ does not verbalize feelings (emotionally repressed)

■ uses primitive defense mechanism of denial (rationalization, minimization)

■ discounts feelings of others

■ thinks he is right, is inflexible, rigid

■ objectifies others

■ defends self, projects blame and responsibility

■ lies, manipulates

■ lacks empathy for others

■ behaves expediently to have own needs met

■ shows low impulse control/low frustration tolerance

■ is aggressive

■ has power and control needs

■ acts possessively (jealous)

■ has difficulty establishing and maintaining relationships (poor social skills)

■ is dependent

■ is hypersexual, sexually demanding

■ appears emotionally needy; wants a caretaker

■ is rigid regarding role differentiation

■ is chauvinistic with sex-role stereotyping

■ is selfish, narcissistic

■ shows concern only for self

Obviously, not all potential abusers share all of
the above-listed traits. Many individuals who exhibit a number of these characteristics do not become abusers. However, abusers do tend to exhibit
many of these traits.

Educational materials and exercises force adult
survivors of double-bind parents to think about, assess, and evaluate their relationships in light of what

constitutes healthy partnerships. At that point, the victim is better equipped to begin to formulate deci- sions for healthy life changes.

These adult victims do best in therapy when three conditions are present. First, they must be ready to make changes. Readiness usually occurs when the victims are vulnerable and the pain of their relationships outweigh secondary gains or pleasure. In other words, they are at a point in life (crisis) when their suffering is genuine and they realize that their customary way of relating to men has not worked. It is time to change or continue in unhappi- ness and misery.

Second, they must have a positive one-on-one relationship with their therapists whose role is to re- parent individuals from dysfunctional backgrounds. It is essential that the therapist provide acceptance, consistency, appropriate role modeling, patience, and guidance.

Finally, a time frame for behavioral change should be implemented. Insights are of little value to abused women in the absence of reality testing.

4

Intentional Game Players: Women With Unresolved Victim Bonding

The victim who has a deep-seated bond to her original perpetrator goes through life with a number of hidden agendas, deriving secondary gains from abusive adult relationships. Often she plays dangerous mind games with her partners in a futile attempt to resolve childhood trauma through repetition.

Relationships are fabricated, lacking authenticity and intimacy, and based on anger, control, manipulation, and needs for power and control. Like her original abuser, this victim has many of the attributes of the antisocial personality, manipulating and objectifying others for her own ends.

For the game player, the world is perceived as unpredictable with need fulfillment only through control of significant others. Often the compulsion to control is so overwhelming that her relationships appear to be addictive.

The underlying dynamic involves a history of childhood sexual abuse during which time the child victim unconsciously identifies with her offender to avoid the victim role. This imprint is replayed again and again in adulthood with attempts to establish control in co-dependent relationships.

Drawn to abusers, the adult victim engages in power plays until she subtly assumes control. Her games often result in rape and battery with her partner's resultant shame and guilt satisfying her power needs. In the end, the male partner loses control and the female is vindicated by his brutality and its accompanying legal and emotional repercussions.

Case Example

Kim, a young woman molested as a child first by her father and later her stepfather, harbored tremendous rage toward men. She felt a need for revenge and control over those who had symbolically hurt her (all men). Having identified with her perpetrators, she was attracted to men with traits similar to her own (e.g. power needs, anger, scorn, and disdain for the opposite sex).

This young woman's first long-term partner, Mark, treated her well during the courtship phase of their relationship. In time, Kim slowly learned behaviors that would trigger Mark's jealously and anger.

After six months, Mark began to slap and shove Kim during arguments. Eventually, he raped and beat her. Kim retaliated by taunting Mark, verbally castrating him and having affairs with other men which she then discussed with him. She felt personal power in hurting him emotionally and in her ability to trigger his anger which escalated to the point where he lost control, further exacerbating his feelings of inadequacy and shame.

Kim remained with Mark until she tired of the game. At age 24, she found another "victim," Bill, who had a shorter fuse than Mark. Bill had a record with the juvenile courts, with three referrals for aggravated assault, simple assault, and assault with a deadly weapon. He had been mandated into anger management courses and knew how to identify anger before it escalated into violent behavior. His plan was to leave the scene at the point when he identified triggers to rage.

Kim felt challenged by Bill, whose approach to her was low-key and laid back, bordering on indifference. He controlled his reactions to her affairs with other men, did not react when she taunted or belittled him, accepted her refusal to have sex with him for weeks or even months, and ignored her nagging and demanding behaviors. When an argument was imminent, he protected himself by leaving her presence.

One night, without provocation or identifiable triggers, Bill beat Kim with a rifle butt while she slept. He then called 911, offering the police no explanation or defense, was arrested and subsequently indicted on a charge of aggravated assault.

Kim spent almost two weeks in the hospital for treatment of internal injuries, contusions, a skull fracture, and a broken arm. When she returned home, she immediately called the office of the District Attorney and begged that the charges against Bill be dismissed so that she could resume her relationship with him.

Kim had won the battle by so enraging Bill that he totally lost control and was humiliated by involvement with the criminal justice system. So powerful was Kim's need for control, retaliation for past offenses, and re-enactment of childhood trauma, that she not only risked her life but sought to do so again.

Psychopathic Maneuver

Character-disordered individuals are unable to tolerate insults to the self, frustration or delayed gratification which elicit unbearable feelings of rage. These feelings must find immediate release which can occur in several ways:

■ Displaced anger — anger vented onto objects or individuals who did not trigger the rage.

■ Passive aggression — anger expressed indirectly through sabotaging some action or event.

■ Direct expression — anger expressed openly, nonviolently or violently, to the individual who triggered the rage.

■ Retaliation — anger in the form of a payback.

It is this last form, retaliation, that constitutes the psychopathic maneuver. Such maneuvers often are chosen by the psychopath who not only releases feelings but emotionally or physically harms the individual who caused the pain.

The psychopath is thought to have experienced a narcissistic injury to the self at an early age. The unhealed wound is reactivated whenever there is a new insult to self. The psychopath's reaction is the same primitive rage experienced when the first injury occurred. The pain is intolerable.

An event occurs that elicits primitive, narcissistic rage that blocks underlying hurt and pain.

⇩

The victim experiences intolerable anxiety, tension, and frustration necessitating immediate relief.

⇩

Retaliation releases rage and provides solace through inflicting hurt.

⇩

The victim immediately experiences calm and is returned to homeostasis.

Case Example

Mark, a spousal abuser court-ordered into therapy for aggravated assault, came to his third session enraged that his wife, Alisha, had sold his stereo equipment to pay the rent. Mark was living temporarily with his parents while Alisha maintained their apartment. He had spent the rent money on a weekend of partying with friends (males and females) and could not understand how Alisha, with whom he was attempting to reconcile, could have sold his favorite possession.

Jealous because Mark was partying with women, Alisha felt uncontrollable rage. Nothing would relieve the mounting tension, frustration, and anger except for a calculated payback. The long-range consequences of her actions did not matter to her. What did matter was revenge for her pain.

Did Alisha have a right to sell the stereo equipment? On one level, perhaps she did. But had she considered the fact that Mark's rage over her actions could result in violent retaliation? Perhaps unconsciously, this is what she had wanted. But, on a conscious level, she knew only that her action would provide temporary relief.

For his part, Mark, upset that the reconciliation with Alisha was "taking too much time," also needed a payback to alleviate his unbearable anguish. Hence, he chose to party, making certain that

Alisha knew what he was doing the weekend in question.

This example illustrates double psychopathic maneuvers and shows clearly how such actions heighten tensions that can result in violent behaviors. These two character-disordered individuals set the stage for increased violence in their relationship. Both lacked impulse control. Neither could tolerate frustration nor consider the long-term consequences for their behaviors and both narcissistically sought immediate relief through retaliation for perceived grievances.

Traits of Antisocial Personalities

■ Superficial charm, affability — lacks depth and genuine caring or concern for others.

■ Manipulation of others — lies and cons others to meet own ends.

■ Problems with authority — resents rules, regulations, and any authority figures.

■ Impulsivity — acts without thinking for immediate-need gratification.

■ Low frustration tolerance — lacks ability to bear emotional pain.

■ Stunted emotional development — emotionally stuck at a young age.

■ Poor social relationships — unable to sustain long-term relationships.

■ Inability to learn from mistakes — repeats behaviors that have a negative impact on self, others, and society.

■ Inability to internalize conflicts — externalizes, acts out, and manipulates.

■ Objectifies others — uses others for own ends.

■ Impaired super-ego development — lacks guilt and remorse for acting-out behaviors.

Therapy for Victims with Unresolved Victim Bonds

Manipulation and power plays dominate the relationships of women with unresolved victim bonds. This generates a constant state of tension and potential violence. The woman identifies herself with her original perpetrator and seeks a partner whom she can objectify, use for her own ends, and ultimately victimize — even at the expense of her own well-being.

Impulsive, reactive, and rageful, she plays her games unpredictably, with little awareness of her behavior. Similarities between the male and female partner in these relationships lead to volatile (and potentially lethal) situations. Often, these relationships result in repetitive, compulsive behaviors, *folie à deux,* and addictive patterns.

Treatment is difficult because there are no secondary gains for victims in these destructive relationships and because there is little suffering to motivate change. The suffering and pain that does exist relates to failed goals rather than a need to extricate the self from unhealthy relationships. It is important for therapists to be aware that these women have many of the attributes of antisocial personalities for which prognoses are guarded.

A woman with unresolved victim bonds are most amenable to therapeutic change when:

■ the relationship has reached a point where she knows she may die, often following life-threatening abuse;

■ the criminal justice system is likely to incarcerate the woman or her partner due to violations of the law;

■ social and economic supports have been removed;

■ authorities, such as protective services, are likely to remove her children; or

■ the male partner, perhaps emotionally healthier than his spouse, has left or may leave the relationship.

The therapist working with victims with unresolved victim bonds should be skilled in dealing with antisocial personalities to preclude client manipulation. These clients will attempt to control the therapeutic situation in the absence of clear direction, goals, contracting, boundary limits, and time frames. Written exercises and chronicling daily progress are helpful in keeping these victims on course and measuring gains.

Written Exercises

Self-Interest

■ Have the client visualize her life five, 10, and 15 years from now if change is not effected and then if positive changes are enacted.

My Life

If I do not change	_If I do change_
In 5 years _____	_In 5 years_ _____
In 10 years _____	_In 10 years_ _____
In 15 years _____	_In 15 years_ _____

■ Have the client list her history of adult male relationships and categorize each as "healthy and functional," "moderately healthy and functional," or "unhealthy and nonfunctional." Have her discuss the patterns. What occurred in her life during these relationships? Was she experiencing unusual stresses, life crises, or significant changes? What will happen if, by age 65, she does not now begin to make changes?

■ Ask the client to list anticipated losses, including social supports, family, children and possibly her life, if she does not alter her patterns of relating to men.

■ Ask the client to list how her behavior has impacted her self-worth with references to school or employment, peers, friends, family, children, and others. How do these people perceive her? How does she perceive herself as an employee, friend, student, daughter, sister, mother? Is she responsible, dedicated, trustworthy, accountable? What needs to happen to improve her relationships? Her self-worth?

Redirection

■ Have the client change her focus in life by understanding that she has a limited amount of energy which she has chosen to expend on maintaining destructive relationships. Explain how this energy can be redirected to obtain social and financial security. Help her develop a strategy by listing the steps she must take that may include:

- additional training/schooling
- church involvement

- civic or community involvement
- renewing family ties

External Authority

■ In the absence of an internalized conscience, these women tend to respond to external controls.

■ Help the client understand that repeated involvement with authorities may result in significant losses, such as incarceration or permanent removal of her children from the home.

Anger Management

■ These victims need to control impulses and tolerate frustration. The cardinal rule is to think before acting.

■ The client should be able to identify:

- triggers to anger
- bodily symptoms indicating that anger is surfacing
- steps to take — e.g. take a walk around the block

Hope

■ Effecting change is difficult, time-consuming, and sometimes frustrating, especially for those victims who are impatient, impulsive, and usually in need of immediate relief when anger or tensions mount.

■ Relief generally takes the form of some action that bypasses rational problem solving.

- feelings (anger, stress, tension) ⇨ action ⇨ current behavior

- feelings ⇨ rational assessment and decision making ⇨ action ⇨ desired behavior.

The client needs to know that long-term gains will outweigh the short-term gratification that comes with the immediacy of these reactions. In the end, she will have greater control due to the operation of cognitive processes.

5

True Victims: Women With Histories of Early Unresolved Trauma

Many adult abuse victims have devastating histories of sexual, physical, and emotional abuse, often beginning in the preschool years and continuing steadily or intermittently through early adulthood. Sometimes, there have been multiple perpetrators within and outside of the home. Usually, these women come from backgrounds that are culturally and economically impoverished, where the living condition is "bread-and-butter" survival.

The resultant damage to the victims, often adult borderline personalities, may be permanent with serious impairments behaviorally, cognitively, emotionally, and psychologically. These women experience anhedonia, where there is no happiness or joy, but rather a chronic state of numbness. They become life's true victims, living periodically on the streets, eking out a meager existence through menial and often degrading jobs, or as regular recipients of public assistance. A number of them fare slightly better, moving from partner to partner with periods of hospitalization for psychogenic or psychiatric illnesses.

The underlying dynamic involves severe disruption in the early developmental stages, resulting in impaired ego and super-ego functions. As children, these women never developed the trust that comes from appropriate bonding or any sense of independence and autonomy. Severe abuse precluded the possibility of the growth of basic trust, and efforts to become self-sufficient were thwarted by parents who were threatened with separation.

It is not uncommon for these true victims to receive disability payments for psychiatric problems, which, coupled with Food Stamps and Aid to Families with Dependent Children (ADFC), enable them to live in relative stability for short periods of time. This group is known to the public as inter- and intragenerational welfare recipients. Abuse of all kinds (sexual, physical, emotional) is so rampant in their lives that it constitutes a cultural norm.

True victims lack a sense of self with almost nonexistent boundaries. What little sense of identity they do have is easily devalued and renounced in their frantic quest to have safety, security, and emotional needs met.

These women have an unhealthy, all-consuming need to be "filled up" by others. To accomplish that end, they will sacrifice themselves, their children, and anything they may possess. Enmeshment and interdependence typify their relationships with partners, parents, and offspring. Usually infantile and emotionally fixated at a young age, they are attention-seeking and people-pleasing, looking for mothering and fathering from authority figures, parents, and children. Crisis-prone, they move through life from one calamity to the next, following the imprint left by their abusive backgrounds. The crises appear to serve as justifications for lack of growth and progress in their lives. During periods that are relatively crisis-free, they often catastrophize with a self-fulfilling prophecy that calamities will continue to dominate their lives.

Trauma stops normal development
⇩
results in regression/fixation with
"badness" as part of identity
⇩
creates a state of vulnerability to abuse.

Sometimes these victims present as hypervigilant and sensitive to perceived threats. However, due to the following characteristics, they tend to seek and attract sadistic, possessive, jealous, and controlling partners:

■ lack of awareness of own needs

■ poor judgment

■ inadequate problem-solving skills

■ values constantly in flux

■ low impulse control

■ low frustration tolerance

Case Example

Shawna, aged 42, is an example of a true victim. She had been married three times and her current husband sexually abused (raped) and belittled her constantly. The marriage ended when two of Shawna's five children alleged that their stepfather, Dale, had molested them. Dale subsequently accepted a plea bargain offered by the courts and served a five-year prison sentence.

Following their marriage, Shawna became involved with a series of abusive males who beat and raped her and coerced her to participate in degrading activities, including *menage à trois*, pornographic filming, and bondage. Eventually, Shawna lost her apartment and children (to protective services) and began living on the streets where she supported her addiction to crack through street prostitution.

Sexually and physically abused since infancy, Shawna could not remember the number of perpetrators who had victimized her. Her history revealed early rape by alcoholic brothers and uncles, often through penetration with sticks and narrow curtain rods which resulted in vaginal scarring and an extensive history of gynecological problems including chronic endometriosis.

Shawna's mother beat her with coat hangers, fly swatters, birch switches, and pots and pans from early childhood, sometimes for minor transgressions but more often randomly, with no precipitating triggers. One of eight children, Shawna was the chosen scapegoat for immediate and extended family members who belittled and criticized her and told her that she deserved whatever physical, sexual, and psychological abuse they inflicted.

Shawna presented as childlike with unmet infantile dependency needs and needs for nuturance, support, and guidance. She lacked boundaries and, in her desperate quest for a giving caretaker, was unable to discriminate among abusers and non-abusers.

During infrequent moments of insight, Shawna would say that she knew she was "sick," thought she was repeating her own abuse, and "didn't know any other way." Frantically attempting to preserve her damaged self-esteem, she projected blame on everyone from protective services (for taking her children), to her spouses, and family of origin. She felt totally helpless in a world she believed to be hostile, uncaring, and overwhelming.

Because of her vulnerability, she attracted sadistic partners with whom she became enmeshed in her never-ending search to please and be loved in return. Feelings of fear and hurt were masked by blunted affect and an air of indifference which further isolated her from those who might feel empathy and reach out to help.

Juanita, 37, another true victim, had a history similar to Shawna's. She, too, experienced early and prolonged physical abuse perpetrated by both parents. Long-term sexual abuse by an aged male neighbor resulted in seductive behavior and further molestation by a school gym teacher and the older brothers of one of her friends.

Like Shawna, Juanita attracted abusive partners from her teenage years through adulthood. Bisexual, she was beaten, controlled, and sexually violated by both males and females. Unlike Shawna, as a young adult, Juanita was able to work and maintain a home for herself and her daughter, Sandy, also a victim of molestation by one of her mother's partners.

When Sandy was five, her mother and several of her male and female peers were arrested for molesting her. Her pre-sentence report from Superior Court revealed that she had sexually abused six young children at the demand of her 56-year-old boyfriend, who used Sandy as a pimp to recruit young victims. He would coerce Juanita to molest the children either sequentially or together while watching and masturbating.

Juanita told her pre-sentence officer that she was not threatened by her boyfriend. Instead, she felt controlled by him and desperately wanted to please him so that he would love her. She fulfilled all of his wishes and even after her arrest, Juanita said that she loved this man and hoped that they would be able to reunite in the future.

Shawna and Juanita, both true victims, shared common characteristics:

- similar backgrounds of extensive, early poly-morphous abuse that resulted in permanent im-pairment of ego functions

- absence of self and blurred boundaries

- merging with partners through enmeshment, in-terdependence, and abulia, or lack of will-power

- vulnerability to controlling, sadistic partners who objectified them for need gratification.

Is therapy effective with such severely dam-aged women? Do they bear any responsibility for their abuse and abusive acts? How should society respond to them? The answers to these questions are difficult but crucial in terms of where society chooses to allocate its ever-dwindling resources for punishment and rehabilitation.

Traits of Women Severely
Abused as Children*

■ Unclear ego boundaries — regresses to helplessness and powerlessness, with possible decompensation or suicide attempts.

■ History of uninterrupted developmental phases — has bonding attachment issues with symbiotic tie to parental figures.

■ Roles limited to abuser, victim, and rescuer — lives in constricted world replete with fantasies.

■ Vulnerability with expectation of mistreatment from others — is conditioned for abuse, use, and degredation.

■ Introjection of "badness" as part of identity — has poor self-esteem, self-hate.

■ Absence of autonomy and independence — has no inner core or self.

■ Mistrust and fear — has predominant emotions of uncertainty, shame, and guilt.

■ Anhedonia — sees world as unsafe with pervasive, blunted feelings.

---

*A number of these women are borderline personalities.

■ Hypervigilance — is watchful yet lacks judgment to distinguish between dangerous and nonthreatening situations.

Therapy for Victims with Histories of Severe, Unresolved Abuse

Victims of severe, prolonged, physical, sexual, and emotional abuse in their families of origin are often marginally functional or nonfunctional with traits of borderline personalities. Conventional psychotherapy may be of value in offering support and unconditional acceptance. Too often, however, these victims become overly attached to their therapists as surrogate mothers and use the treatment process for ventilation and reinforcement of repeated dysfunctional behaviors. Sometimes, transference is operating; other times, the clients, usually crisis-prone, are manipulative or attention-seeking with severe abandonment issues.

Therapists may become "hooked" (countertransference) by responding to the neediness or situational and interpersonal crises of these women without consideration of the importance of positive, measurable outcomes in therapy.

These victims certainly need help, but tend to do best with social casework services that directly address the multiple dysfunctions impacting every aspect of their lives. Many of them desperately need resources and referrals.

Unfortunately, social service systems, impersonal and bureaucratic, frustrate the victims who, too often, do not follow through with referrals. Caseworkers may be called upon to "walk the client through" these systems by accompanying them for services and/or providing transportation.

Social Casework Services for Victims of Severe Abuse

- Shelter care ....battered women's shelters, shelters for the homeless, government housing, YWCA

- Food, clothing.............Salvation Army, Goodwill Industries, food stamps, Aid to Families with Dependent Children (AFDC)

- Disability ....state agencies

- Support to protect ....Parents Anonymous children from abuse

- Stress daycare ....protective services for children

- Placement for...............child crisis centers, protective children   services

- Therapy......................battered women's and rape crisis hotlines for referrals

- Restraining orders,........police departments in cities where orders of protection   offenses occurred

- Victim assistance.........district or county attorneys (support, financial)   offices

- Support groups.............AA, NA, publicly-funded nonprofit agencies

- Employment................welfare offices, vocational
rehabilitation

- Medication....................Medicare, Medicaid

- Education.....................local high-schools for G.E.D.;
community colleges for loans,
grants, and training programs

The caseworker's approach should be firm, directive, and supportive to counter-act the tendency of these women to receive attention through manipulation and repeated crises.

Although the prognosis for change tends to be poor, some clients do stabilize and benefit from the various support systems to which they have been referred. In these instances, the victims may be ready to benefit from individual psychotherapy, provided that:

■ a time-frame for therapy is firmly established

■ treatment goals are clearly established

■ there is an agreement between the client and therapist that the client will continue to receive services established through casework intervention, such as job or school referrals, or attendance at AA, NA, and so forth

■ a coordinated, inter-agency approach is implemented to prevent manipulation since the victims tend to repeat childhood dysfunctions by

creating conflicts among their various caseworkers and therapists

Goals for Time-Limited Psychotherapy with Victims of Severe Abuse

■ Support and encouragement through active listening and allowing for ventilation.

■ Stress management.

■ Education in the following areas:

  • abusive relationships and the cycle of abuse

  • secondary gains victims often derive from
    abusive relationships

  • the relationship between abusive histories
    and violent adult relationships

  • parenting/parent education with a focus on
    bonding, roles, boundaries, and the protec-
    tion of children

  • repetition of childhood scripts that invalidate
    the self and self-worth

  • dependence and the script that women are
    worthless without partners

  • the counter-productiveness of fear, guilt and
    catastrophizing

- secondary gains from crisis-prone lifestyles

- healthy, functional relationships

■ Practice in the use of affirmations and aphorisms (Halpern 1983).

■ Concrete goal-setting and contracting for positive change.

■ Techniques to use for counter-acting fears and flashbacks such as self-statements ("This is now and I am here now; this is not then when I was small and powerless").

■ Self-exploration exercises to strengthen fragmented selves such as, "I am . . . , I like . . . , I want . . . , I was . . ."

■ Reinforcement for progress and behavioral gains.

■ Reflection and feedback on reality testing with new relationships.

Part Three:
Special Considerations

6
General Concerns With Abused Women

There are six features somewhat unique to battered children that have a strong impact on their relationships as adults. Since these features, originating in childhood, strongly predispose to abusive relationships, they merit separate and detailed attention.

These features are:

- Externalization
- Anger
- Attachment
- Traumatic Bonding
- Addiction
- Learned Helplessness and Battered Women's Syndrome

Everyone experiences anger and people externalize, manipulate, or have histories of attachment problems in varying degrees. What is unique about adult victims is the degree to which they experience these symptoms and how these issues directly affect relationships with significant others.

Externalization or Other Orientedness

A common theme among adults who were sexually, physically, and emotionally abused as children is their tendency to seek fulfillment outside of themselves. This results from painful childhoods when the emerging self was injured and insulted.

These women were defined by others when they were very young. Self-worth was determined by abusive or mentally ill parents. Love was a conditional commodity but there were no guidelines regarding what these conditions were or how to meet them. Miller (1989) refers to externalization and dependence of someone outside for self-definition. In other words, without "other," there is no self.

Most of the characteristics of abused women relate to this central feature (absence of a strong sense of self). Without "self," other becomes essential for survival and any price is paid to fill the empty, panic-stricken void. Values are secondary; trust is bestowed without thought or evaluation; relationships are fabricated and reality is distorted or replaced by fantasy or illusion.

It is easy for women abused as children to abnegate the fragile self following their childhood im-

prints. When the parent abused them, they withdrew
into fantasy, denied reality, and became covert par-
ticipants (and often caretakers) in the game playing
in their sick families.

For these women as children, there was no
communication or authenticity. Rather, their lives
were filled with hypocrisy and deception and they
were taught to manipulate and comply simply to
survive. Their credo ("don't think, don't talk, don't
trust, and don't feel") followed them to and through
adulthood.

Anger

Adults who have been sexually, physically,
and psychologically abused as children are angry,
even rageful. They were conditioned as children to:

- be hurt
- feel anger and rage about that hurt
- suppress anger because demonstrations of
  anger resulted in retaliation

What does the adult with a background of severe abuse do with stored and suppressed rage? She
has several choices, each of which provides a secondary gain or pay-off, but none which is either
healthy or functional.

Behavior	Pay-off
• turns anger on self through self-destructive acting out such as suicide, anorexia, self- mutilation	• allows victim to be rescued; • helps maintain victim role; • is punishment for internalized "bad self"
• turns anger on self by setting up others to victimize her	• allows victim to be rescued; • helps maintain victim role; • is punishment for internalized "bad self"
• displaces anger in criminal acts (shoplifting, violent behavior)	• becomes perpetrator, not victim; • allows legitimatized punishment for internalized "bad self"
• retaliates through perpetration	• evens the score; facilitates retaliation; • allows legitimatized punishment for internalized "bad self"
• maintains angry, aggressive life posture	• covers up fear, hurt, sadness, and despair; may prevent psychological decompensation; • allows social isolation, thus validating low self-worth and "bad self"
• expresses anger passive-aggressively	• helps victims maintain ambivalence about anger yet vent some negative feelings

The above behaviors graphically indicate how vulnerable these adults are to dangerous situations. The women are limited to the roles of victim, rescuer, and perpetrator, both of whom they are and whom they seek as significant others. Anger turned inward results in life-threatening situations or victimization by others; displaced anger and acting-out behaviors result in punishment and abuse; and passive-aggressive manifestations inevitably backfire by inciting rage and frustration in others.

Case Example

Janine is an example of an adult victimized as a child, who suppressed anger, first at her original abusers and later at her abusive partners. Physically and sexually abused as a child, Janine blocked the painful feelings associated with the molestation and denied feeling angry about the beatings inflicted by her mother throughout her childhood.

Following her childhood script, Janine chose a partner with traits similar to those of her father. James was authoritarian in the home but ineffectual in the world of work with multiple employment problems. He drank heavily and, when drunk, beat his wife.

At first, Janine blamed herself for the abuse and tried harder to please her spouse. Over time, she sunk into a deep depression and functioned with the aid of Zoloft, prescribed by her family physician,

The beatings became more severe and increased in frequency with the passage of time. Along with battering, James began to abuse his wife sexually by forced sodomy and inordinate demands that the couple engage in intercourse two to three times daily.

James was compulsive about the household and issues related to grooming, cleanliness, and personal appearance. He belonged to a gym and worked out three times per week to maintain a healthy physique despite his alcohol abuse.

As James' demands for an immaculate home increased, his wife became more and more lax in her performance of household chores. She also gained 25 pounds in one year, wore no make-up, and dressed shabbily. Most of the couple's arguments, often resulting in abuse, centered around issues of personal appearance and home maintenance. James would call his wife a "slut" and a "dirtbag" as he screamed about her unkempt appearance and lack of tidiness in the home.

Part of Janine's problem regarding cleanliness, appearance, and weight gain probably resulted from chronic depression. On the other hand, she fully understood that there was a direct relationship between those issues and James's battery. Furthermore, she dressed appropriately at her secretarial job and maintained a well-kept office.

Was Janine setting herself up to be victimized? Proving that she was worthless? Expressing passive-aggressive anger by unconsciously choosing to enrage her spouse about issues she knew were vitally important to him?

It is likely that all three factors motivated her behavior — depression, self-sabotage, and passive-aggressive expression of anger. Secondary gains aside, Janine's behavior was highly dysfunctional and served merely to exacerbate her spouse's anger and abuse.

Attachment

Impaired attachment plays a very significant role in abusive relationships. Attachment problems affect the overall style of relating for some women victimized as children as well as the specific reactions these victims experience when there is perceived loss or abandonment.

Halpern (1983) links a phenomenon referred to as attachment hunger to the addictive quality of dysfunctional relationships. When the following two conditions exist, victims experience inordinate emotional needs that override the operation of rational thought processes. This occurs when there is:

■ a childhood history of impaired or faulty gratification of attachment needs during infancy (symbiotic phase of development). The infant's early need to bond is disrupted or impaired by abusive, or mentally or emotionally ill parents. There might be outright abandonment, double-bind reactions, or neglect by the parents. In some cases, external factors such as family illness, hospitalization, or removal of the child by protective services may be responsible for the disrupted or impaired bonding.

■ parenting problems resulting from an inability to "let go" or encourage autonomy in the growing infant (separation-individuation phase of development). Because of their own fear of abandonment, these parents of adult victims encourage continued symbiosis and enmeshment with their youngsters and are very threatened by their children's move toward independence.

The imprints left by attachment problems are enduring and create tremendous vulnerability in adults. Without treatment, these adult children are destined to have, at best, maladaptive relationships and, at worst, violent and abusive ones. Halpern (1983) refers to the feelings of children with attachment problems (fear of abandonment and quest for need gratification, e.g., "the ever-flowing breast") as powerful, primitive, and lodged in bodily reactions and body chemistry.

Women with attachment problems repeat patterns established in childhood, transfer feelings from parent to spouse, and operate as abandoned infants, dichotomizing the good and bad mother with love and hate when needs are not met (Halpern 1983).

These women are dominated by the need for symbiotic, interdependent relationships. Their relationships are characterized by self-defeating, often abusive attachments that reflect low self-worth,

fears, and insecurity. Extreme emotions, similar to
those of the infant, dominate their reactions to significant others whether it be despair, fear, anxiety,
passivity, or hopelessness at the prospect of abandonment. Without therapy, these women remain
emotionally stuck at the infantile stage of relationships and are vulnerable to abuse.

Symbiotic Phase	Separation-Individuation Phase
Parent-infant attachment problem stemming from psychopathology of parent or from external factors	Inability of parent to "let go" for independence and autonomy in child

Child has inordinate needs; cannot function
independently; has impaired sense of self;
experiences blurred boundaries; fears abandonment
⇩
Adult carries childhood imprint; has low
self-worth; transfers feelings for parent to partner;
is fixated at need-fulfillment stage; fears
abandonment
⇩
For need fulfillment, adult relinquishes self, power,
control; seeks addictive relationships and becomes
vulnerable to abuse by partner

Beverly James also writes at length about attachment problems and relates trauma to attachment. Traumatic experiences result in disturbed
attachment and attachment trauma (James 1994).

James refers to the alarm-numbing response of children with attachment problems and this phenomenon has particular bearing on abused women. Simplified, what occurs is as follows:

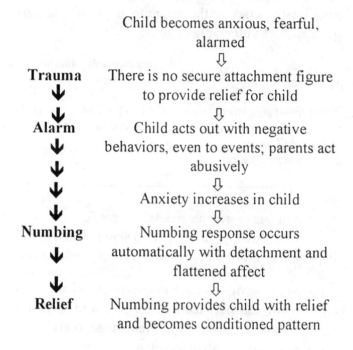

Child becomes anxious, fearful, alarmed
⇩
Trauma   There is no secure attachment figure
↓   to provide relief for child
↓   ⇩
Alarm   Child acts out with negative
↓   behaviors, even to events; parents act
↓   abusively
↓   ⇩
↓   Anxiety increases in child
↓   ⇩
Numbing   Numbing response occurs
↓   automatically with detachment and
   flattened affect
↓   ⇩
Relief   Numbing provides child with relief
   and becomes conditioned pattern

This childhood imprint is relevant to the later responses of abuse adults. For relief from pain, anxiety, and depression, victims become provocative and antagonistic so that anxiety is heightened, resulting in the automatic response of numbness and relief.

It is easy to see how these reactions are conducive to and encourage abuse. A woman who is anxious and fearful seeks relief. By generating a negative and abusive dynamic with her partner (pushing his buttons), she becomes more agitated and fearful until the numbing response kicks in and provides her with much-needed relief.

Sandy's mother abandoned her to her incestuous father when she was 18 months old. Dad began molesting her at two and the abuse continued until her tenth year when her teacher, suspicious about Sandy's chronic stomachaches and unkempt appearance, referred her to the school nurse who learned about the molestation and reported the case to protective services.

Placed with an aunt, Sandy ran away frequently in her teen years and, finally, at the age of 14, was placed in a state-operated group home where she remained until the age of 17. Sandy then found employment first as a cocktail waitress and then as a bartender. She abused alcohol and marijuana, occasionally shoplifting, and, by age 25, had had 17 sexual partners.

Her relationships with men followed a pattern. There was an immediate attraction and idealization of her partners followed by indifference and boredom. Men were chosen for some external feature that appealed to Sandy at the time — appearance, money, employment. She sought excitement, thrills, and had an inordinate narcissistic need to be the center of attention.

This young woman never really knew her boyfriends. She played a role with the men who were objects for her pleasure. In order to maintain the relationships and remain "the most important person" in her partners' lives, she patterned her behavior after theirs with similar interests and goals. If John liked to fish, Sandy fished; if Jim liked hard rock, Sandy listened to hard rock. Chameleon-like, she had no core identity.

Because of her neediness and lack of self, Sandy began to attract domineering abusive males. At first, the abuse was psychological. Her partners lacked respect for her; forgot to call before arriving at her home; insisted on frequent sex; did not take her to the movies or restaurants; and made frequent references to her as a "bar slut" and "nymph."

Eventually, men began to abuse Sandy physically, with a gradual escalation in violence until the day she found herself in intensive care with a serious skull fracture, following an episode when her partner knocked her against a stone fence.

Motivated by narcissistic needs, she lacked a core self. Abandoned by her protector as a child, her attachment issues were further compounded by the molestation by her father, also a protector who abandoned her psychologically. Self-absorbed and a role player, her childhood imprints precluded any possibility of her experiencing functional relationships based on mutuality, respect, trust, genuine care, and concern for her partner.

Traumatic Bonding

Whether the adult female victim suffers from double-blind parenting, is a game player, or true victim, she may develop a trauma bond with her perpetrator. Dutton (1995) believes that traumatic bonding occurs for two reasons:

- the fact that the abuser has more power than the victim,

- the fact that the abuse is intermittent. Learning theory postulates that periodically reinforced behaviors are more difficult to extinguish).

What occurs with traumatic bonding is a loyalty by the victim similar to the attachment that sometimes occurs between hostages and victims. The phrase, Stockholm Syndrome, was coined following a crime in Sweden when a bank teller, held hostage by a robber, fell in love with her captor. To survive and feel empowered, the victim unconsciously identified with her perpetrator.

Jones (1994) describes the Stockholm Syndrome as spontaneous identification under stress. The powerful offender allows his victim to survive and the woman bonds with her abuser through pathological transference. The Stockholm Syndrome is a combination of psychological infantilism (being "scared stiff") and pathological transference.

Traumatic Bond
Brainwashing, Power Imbalance

Victim	Abuser
anxiety, depression, worthlessness	omnipotence
⇩	⇩
bonds with "nice" part of abuser and dissociates and isolates abuse	depends on victim for sense of power
	⇩
	is nice to victim to maintain her loyalty

Traumatic bonding helps to explain why victims find it difficult to leave abusive environments, protect perpetrators, and excuse and minimize their behaviors. It also helps to explain why they return to abusive homes and seek reconciliation at any cost.

In an earlier chapter on double-bind, or intentional game players with unresolved victim bonding, the case of Kim and Bill was described. Bill nearly killed Kim one night when he was experiencing dissociative rage. Despite the clear and imminent threat to her life, Kim wanted to reconcile with Bill to gain the ultimate power of destroying him.

It appeared that Kim had identified with her original offender and subsequent abusers and had become a perpetrator in the convoluted relationship involved in domestic violence. This interpretation is slightly different from the usual explanation for traumatic bonding.

Traumatic Bond

Victim   **Abuser**

identifies with perpetrator   omnipotence
⇩   ⇩
bonds with "bad" part of   depends on victim for sense
abuser and seeks payback   of power
and retaliation for original
abuse   ⇩

                                    terrorizes victim intermittently
                                    to maintain control

Kim identified with her original offender and subsequent abusers and had become a perpetrator in the twisted interplay involved in domestic violence.

Original abuser victimizes
⇩
Child victim identifies with abuser for
power and survival
⇩
Adult victim seeks original abuser in
partner, identifies with abuser
⇩
Adult victim is abused, needs to retaliate
⇩
Adult victim sets up abuser to re-offend
and suffer the consequences
⇩
Adult victim feels empowered

Learned Helplessness and the Battered Woman's Syndrome

It is this author's contention that (1) learned helplessness may be part of the problem for domestic violence, not just for battered women, but for harassed employees; children who protect parents; parents who do not report violent children to authorities, and so forth; (2) learned helplessness alone does not explain the complex web of entanglement involved in abusive relationships. It is one effect only, an effect particularly predictable for true victims of violence. Game players and psychopathic females do not appear to suffer from this syndrome.

However, Lenore Walker's "Battered Woman's Syndrome" (1979) has widely been accepted as a general explanation for why women remain in abusive relationships. For this reason, a brief description of this syndrome is presented.

The theory of learned helplessness postulates that due to a number of sociological variables, including the perception of women in society, and sex-role socialization/stereotyping, the battered woman feels a lack of control, powerlessness, and psychological paralysis regarding her welfare. This perception leads to a state of learned helplessness with a resultant inability to end the abusive relationship (Straus 1975).

Learned helplessness, which is the core of the Battered Woman's Syndrome, is associated with a cluster of symptoms, including passivity, apathy, lack of motivation, problem-solving deficits, depression, and anxiety (Launis and Lindquist 1988).

One study of battered women revealed that the subjects were unable to perceive alternatives to their plight and generally were avoidant and dependent (Launis and Lindquist 1988). Walker likens abused women to the subject of controlled experimentation who receives a repeated series of electric shocks (Straus 1975). Soon, as a result of learned helplessness, the woman's motivation to respond is diminished and she becomes passive and hopeless. She loses her cognitive ability to perceive success and cannot foresee successful resolution to her pain. Motivation ceases as her behavioral and emotional repertoire become increasingly more constricted. The end result is a state of hopeless paralysis.

Cycle of Abuse

Tension-building phase: minor battering; verbal
abuse by the male; appeasement by the
female which leads the male to think
he can intensify violence

⇩

Acute battering: the female lacks control
and feels trapped; the male has power

⇩

Repentence: contrition, relief, and
illusion of forgiveness for both parties

Walker (1990) lists five factors in childhood and seven in adulthood that predispose to learned helplessness.

For children, these factors are:

- sexual abuse
- situations where the child lacks control, such as poverty, divorce, death, and chemical abuse by parents
- sex-role stereotyping and rigid, traditional socialization
- health problems or chronic illness
- witnessing or experiencing battering in the home

For adults, these factors are:

- cycle of violence
- sexual abuse
- psychological torture
- intrusiveness of batterer, including jealousy and possessiveness
- isolation of women
- chemical abuse by either partner
- violence correlates (children, pets, objects)

Learned helplessness is one effect of battery and certainly applies to women victimized all of their lives in a nonsupportive emotional and social climate. However, applying this theory to all battered women is an oversimplification of the complex interrelationships that exist between victims and offenders.

Addiction

Often, the addictive quality of victim-perpetrator relationships is intense and, when seen as such, helps clarify why these women find it difficult to separate from their partners. These are the relationships based on dependence, co-dependence, and interdependence with enmeshment and blurred boundaries.

Addictive relationships share certain features, among them:

■ the inability to dissolve the relationship despite rational reasons for doing so

■ rationalizations to justify remaining in the relationship

■ acute anxiety and panic when contemplating termination of the relationship

■ severe withdrawal when attempts to leave the relationship are made

■ feelings of liberation once the relationship has ended (unlike the grief experienced once functional relationships end)

■ relationship based on dependence, not choice (Halpern 1983).

The addiction is an unconscious attempt to relieve loneliness, fear of abandonment, emptiness, and boredom with a fantasized bond that becomes obsessive (Peabody 1989). Addictive relationships are predicated on preoccupations and obsessions that provide a temporary fix.

Unfortunately, the addict soon becomes obsessed, controlling, and dependent. She uses the relationship to measure her self-worth, is unable to set limits, isolates from others, and tries to fuse with her partner. These feelings place the relationship in jeopardy and bestow power on the potential abuser who may become angry and take advantage of his partner's vulnerability.

Increasingly insecure, the victim may somaticize her anger with psychosomatic illnesses or she may abuse drugs and alcohol to anesthetize her feelings. She seeks the "rush" or "high," the constant fulfillment. Her feelings are unmodulated and polarized into the extremes of euphoria or despair; rage or numbness (Peabody 1989).

Addictive Relationships*

infatuation idealization fantasies illusions euphoria	⇨	addiction triggered with obsessions and fantasies	⇨	deterioration of relation-ships, decline of rein-forcing effects of relationships

	⇨	stress, alcohol, drugs, and illness followed by termi-nation of the rela-tionship	⇨	cycle begins again

The origin of addictive relationships relates to disrupted attachment and dependency bonds in childhood. The result is a ravaging hunger for de-pendent attachment in adulthood. Victims are drawn to adults, who, like their parents, trigger their addic-tive tendencies for need fulfillment (Peabody 1989).

---

*From S. Peabody. *Addiction to Love: Overcoming Obsession and Dependency in Relationships.*

7
A Word About the Abuser

It should be clear from the foregoing chapters that emotional, sexual, and physical battery do not occur in isolation. There are specific triggers to violence, along with immediate and long-range predisposing psychological and personality factors for both partners. Abuse, though a behavioral choice of the perpetrator, involves a pathological relationship with the victim.

While this book has focused on the victim, a brief description of the typical batterer should prove helpful to professional and lay people in their efforts to understand and deal with the phenomenon of domestic violence.*

The typical abusive male has power and control needs predicated on stereotypic beliefs in male supremacy. Outwardly, he may appear charming

*An excellent and thorough study of abusers can be found in D. G. Dutton, *The Batterer: A Psychological Profile.* N.Y.: Basic Books, 1995.

and likable, careful to commit violent or psychologically abusive acts in secrecy. A number of these men, like their female counterparts, are antisocial personalities. In Dutton's sample, 40 percent of the abusers were character-disordered (1995).

Repressed with shallow emotional responses, a limited emotional repertoire, and emotional self-alienation, these men present like young toddlers in adult bodies with unresolved rage from their own childhood traumas (Robertson 1992).* Robertson lists eight traits of the Emotionally Repressed Male (ERM):

- masked low self-esteem

- co-dependence

- self-centeredness

- addictive personality

- history of family violence

- control and power issues

- deceit and denial

- isolation

The typical abuser lacks maturity and self-confidence, is insecure and jealous. To feel adequate

---

*A solid resource for abusive couples by a former batterer is R. Robertson, *Confessions of an Abusive Husband: A How-to-Book for "Abuse Free" Living for Everyone.* Lake Oswego, OR: Heritage Park Publishing Co., 1992.

and meet his dependency needs, he psychologically enslaves his victim and annihilates her self-worth. He needs his partner, just as she needs him, to complete his sense of self with unconscious attempts to fuse her personality with his.* He controls to possess her.

Gelles notes that batterers are often under-achievers whose partners may be more successful academically, financially, and vocationally. He reports that in homes where spousal abuse occurs, 69 percent of the wives were more educated than their husbands and 62 percent had a higher occupational status. Over 80 percent of the abusers had low status jobs such as laborer or truck driver (Gelles 1987). Many of these men are dreamers with unrealistic plans for the future.

Broken dreams, unfulfilled expectations, self-pity, and bitterness exacerbate their anger, paranoia, and morbid jealousy directed toward their wives. They project blame and feelings of inadequacy and failure, and scapegoat their wives, calling them inflammatory names such as slut and whore. Violence reaffirms their male status and keeps their personalities intact.

Like his female counterpart, the batterer may have experienced childhood abuse and neglect. A national sample by Straus, Gelles, and Steinmetz (1980) found that men who witnessed violence be-

---

*Note the similarities in features of both abusers and victims whose relationships are often based on complementary bonds.

tween their parents were three times more likely to hit their wives. The sons of the most violent parents had rates of wife abuse 1,000 times greater than the sons of nonviolent parents.

A recent review of the literature on spousal abuse indicated that 69 percent of the empirical studies found an association between wife battery and being beaten as a child (reported in Browne 1987). Thus, these men are both perpetrators and victims. Like their partners, they alternately fear abandonment and engulfment with attachment issues dating back to childhood.

Typically, abusers experience a three-phase cycle of abuse. First, there is the tension-building when the abuser ruminates, projects, and inflicts minor injuries or verbal assaults on his partner. Second, there is acute battering with the infliction of serious injuries. During this phase, Dutton reports that the men may dissociate and experience an altered state of consciousness similar to that experienced by their victims. Also, they may become addicted to the release of tension and anxiety following escalated violence.

The final honeymoon phase involves relief, transient guilt, and contrition before the cycle begins to repeat itself. Dutton (1995) refers to the after-effects of violence as seductive, involving the collusion of both partners in an illusory state of permanent calm.

As with victims, batterers come from every ethnic and socioeconomic class. They all experience anomie, or a breakdown of social norms and values. About 15 percent experience sexual arousal during violent acts (Davidson 1978). Alcohol and drugs are associated with battery and may be contributory factors since they lower inhibitions. Browne (1987) reports on one study indicating that 73 percent of abused women reported alcohol abuse by their spouses. However, chemicals are not causative factors (Davidson 1978).

Batterers share a number of traits with their victims including similar childhood histories, fluctuating roles, chemical abuse, and problems with self-esteem and anger. However, a single distinguishing feature separates the offender from the victim — the batterer chooses to abuse another human being and bears sole responsibility for his actions.

Traits of Batterers

- power and control needs
- stereotypic view of women
- rigid, traditional roles
- sex-role stereotyping; confusion of sex with intimacy
- superficial charm
- manipulation
- expedience
- repressed emotions

- shallow emotional responses
- emotional self-alienation
- limited emotional and behavioral repertoire
- history of abuse
- history of violent acting out
- chemical abuse
- regression
- low self-worth
- co-dependence/dependence
- self-centeredness/narcissism
- addiction
- deceit
- denial, minimization, rationalization
- immaturity
- jealousy
- insecurity, feelings of inadequacy
- anger
- underachievement
- projection, blame, displacement as defenses
- fears of abandonment and engulfment
- poor communication
- absence of empathy
- isolation
- avoidance of conflicts
- poor stress management

8
Conclusion: Healthy, Survivor, or Victim?

What causes some women unconsciously to seek abusers while others instinctively avoid them? Of course, instinct is based on honed intuition, knowledge, and an ability to sense the total gestalt of another person.

Women who avoid abusers operate from a position of healthy self-interest, awareness of secondary verbal and nonverbal cues about a potential partner, and knowledge about the dangers of control, chemical abuse, and male inadequacy. Shared goals and values are primary motivators for establishing connections with a potential partner.

Healthy women establish relationships slowly over time with understanding that knowing another person is a process that involves trust, honesty, and commitment rather than ownership. These women have impulse control, are able to function inde-

pendently, and readily "let go" of dysfunctional relationships.

Healthy women do not want to change or fix
anyone. They seek actuality, not potential. They live
in reality, not fantasy. They settle for nothing less
than equality and parallel growth rather than co-dependence and enmeshment with their partners. Secure in themselves and relying on a solid foundation
for their relationships, they are neither jealous nor
insecure.

These women have no need to anesthetize or
medicate themselves with chemicals and do not
block or suppress painful emotions. They do not
seek a "fix" or "high." The self is intact and does
not require constant replenishment.

Women abused as children do not have the
same tools as healthy women. Coming from chaotic
and dysfunctional backgrounds, they lack appropriate role models and do not have the knowledge or
understanding to differentiate between what is normal and what is not normal. Propelled by affective
needs and operating with the handicap of affective
dyscontrol, they rush into relationships with emotional neediness. Cognitive operations such as
evaluation and judgment are suspended.

The repetitive, patterned behavior of these
women seduces others to reinforce their victim identity. They are magnets for abusers. Manipulative, in-
herently dishonest, and chameleon-like, they can as

easily operate from the script of offender, victim, or rescuer, depending on which role is most advantageous at the time.

As angry offenders, they play intentional games, manipulating others, and unconsciously using anger to preclude the possibility of intimacy and vulnerability. These victims use anger either as a payback for retaliation against original offenders, or they operate from childhood scripts when they identified with their perpetrators.

True victims are the perpetual children, martyrs, and scapegoats who unconsciously abdicate responsibility for their life decisions. As child victims of severe abandonment, they are unpredictable, approaching and avoiding intimacy with failed attempts at self-protection of a threatened marginal self.

Adults less severely abused as children also suffer from the effects of dysfunctional backgrounds, especially if they received mixed messages from their parents. These women have unresolved identity issues and intense mood shifts. Relationships with their partners are characterized by splitting, transient intensity followed by devaluation and overall instability.

Knowledge about the devastation of abusive backgrounds facilitates an understanding of the ravaging effects these histories have on adult relationships in general, and on the violent ones in particular. Understanding the differences in these abusive backgrounds and the subsequent manifestations and symptoms that result from these differences, facilitates therapeutic interventions and allows treatment providers to distinguish among appropriate and inappropriate modalities, to distinguish which women are treatable and which are not.

Appendix A
Continuum of Abuse by Types

(least → functional → functional woman
vulnerable) woman with no with or without abuse
history of abuse history (abuse not
prolonged in child-
hood); victim of
misfortune

non-functional → non-functional → nonfunctional woman
woman with his- woman with his- with history of severe,
tory of double- tory of unresolved prolonged abuse;
bind parenting victim-bond; in- true victim
in family of tentional game
origin; uninten- player
tional game player

→ (most vulnerable)

Continuum of

	Healthy Woman; No History of Abuse	Victim of Misfortune
Functioning	Functional	Functional
Relationship	Healthy, based on reciprocity	Potentially healthy; motivated to change
Key Traits	Ego integration; sense of self; boundaries	Ego integration; confusion; able to grow
Diagnoses	No pathology	Variable; no major pathology
Prognoses	Excellent	Good
Therapy	Not needed	Short-term, reality-based, educational

Abuse by Types

Victim of Double-Blind Parents	Victim of Unresolved Family Bond	Victim of Severe Abuse
Dysfunctional	Dysfunctional	Dysfunctional
Unhealthy; unintentional game player	Unhealthy; intentional game player	Unhealthy with alternating victim, offender, rescuer roles
Poor role models; confused about what is normal	Identification with offender; addictive; repeats early trauma	Infantile; fixated at young age; blurred boundaries
May have border-line features	Possible anti-social personality	May have border-line personality
May be good	Guarded	Poor
Cognitive educational	Reality-based; appeal to self-interest	Social casework; short-term, goal-oriented

Appendix B
Childhood Imprints

1) Healthy Woman (no history of abuse)

    A. Relations: was taught healthy relationships in family of origin

    B. World view: perceives world as challenging; experiences wide range of appropriate emotions and behaviors

    C. Boundaries: has strong boundaries; is able to integrate thoughts and feelings; thinks, then acts; has strong sense of self

    D. Roles: had good role models; is aware of needs and feelings

    E. Functioning: makes choices in accordance with values and goals; is assertive, independent, and goal-oriented

2) Victim of Misfortune (may or may not have history of abuse)

    A. Relations: understands how healthy relations operate

    B. World view: feels confusion but is motivated to change and grow

    C.   Boundaries: has adequate boundaries with sense of self

    D.   Roles: had adequate role models

    E.   Functioning: understands assertiveness and independence; has some ambivalence regarding self-assertion

3)   Victim of Double-Bind Parenting in Family of Origin

    A.   Relations: has approach-avoidance reaction to relationships; fears engulfment and abandonment

    B.   World view: lives in world of fantasies, illusions, and potentials

    C.   Boundaries: boundaries either too rigid or flexible with same person; compartmentalizes relationships; trusts too easily or not at all

    D.   Roles: is confused regarding what is normal and not normal; is unable to discriminate properly

    E.   Functioning: generalizes from the particular, but inappropriately; is inconsistent; unintentionally plays games

4)   Victim with History of Unresolved Bond in Family of Origin

A. Relations: has unauthentic, fabricated relationships based on anger, control, and need for power; addictive relationships

B. World view: sees world as unpredictable; needs must be met through power and control

C. Boundaries: identifies with perpetrator; plays games; repeats childhood trauma; is reactive and impulsive; sees love as conditional

D. Roles: chameleon; plays roles that provide greatest benefit

E. Functioning: self-centered; operates for need fulfillment; retaliates when hurt

5) Victim with History of Severe, Prolonged Abuse

A. Relations: renounces fragile self to please others; is frantic to have safety needs met

B. World view: perceives world as hostile, terrifying; experiences anhedonia, emptiness, hollowness, and blunted affect

C. Boundaries: no sense of self or boundaries

D. Roles: only knows roles of victim-offender-rescuer

E. Functioning: emotionally stuck at an early age; devalues self; has poor judgment; is infantile, attention-seeking and crisis-prone

Appendix C
Additional Exercises for
Adult Battered Women

1) Power, Control, and Coercion

   Analyze your relationships with adult males using the following scale:

   A. He likes me to do things his way

   ☐ Never

   ☐ Sometimes

   ☐ Usually

   ☐ Always

   B. He makes most of the important decisions for us

   ☐ Never

   ☐ Sometimes

   ☐ Usually

   ☐ Always

   C. He does not understand me

   ☐ Never

❑   Sometimes

❑   Usually

❑   Always

D.   My needs are unimportant to him

❑   Never

❑   Sometimes

❑   Usually

❑   Always

E.   He prevents me from growing as a person with independent interests and friends

❑   Never

❑   Sometimes

❑   Usually

❑   Always

F.   He puts me down and criticizes me

❑   Never

❑   Sometimes

❑   Usually

❑   Always

G. When I don't do what he wants, he threat-
ens me verbally

❑ Never

❑ Sometimes

❑ Usually

❑ Always

H. He feels that women should be "put in
their place"

❑ Never

❑ Sometimes

❑ Usually

❑ Always

The above methods of power and coercion are
signs of abuse, demonstrating control needs and attempts to reduce victims to nonentities. If you an-
swered positively to any of the above, consider the
reasons (pay-offs) why you remain in the relationship.

2) Values, Clarification, and Decision Making

Emotions and emotional needs tend to dominate and direct the behavior of abused women.
The pre-eminence of emotional needs, coupled
with inadequate education regarding values,

contributes to the vulnerability of adults with histories of double-bind parenting. Begin thinking about your relationships with the following exercise:

Leaving or Staying in an Abusive Relationship

Answer "yes" or "no" to the following statements:

A.   We share common values and goals
     _____.

B.   I am satisfied with the relationship
     _____.

C.   I love him, not his potential _____.

D.   I do not want or expect him to change
     _____.

E.   I find myself excusing his behavior _____.

F.   I need him, not want him _____.

G.   He cares about me and my needs _____.

H.   He cares about my personal growth
     _____.

I.   He encourages me to have outside interests, friends, career _____.

J. I really can trust him _____.

K. He really cares for me, not how I make him feel _____.

L. We know one another very well _____.

M. He makes me feel good about myself _____.

N. He respects women and believes in gender equality _____.

O. He does not like pornography or anything else that degrades women _____.

P. He is macho with all male interests _____.

Q. He thinks homosexuals are disgusting _____.

R. He thinks about sex all the time _____.

S. He does not criticize or belittle me _____.

T. He would never physically or sexually abuse me _____.

U. He wants sex all the time _____.

V. He thinks we should make up after arguing by having sex _____.

W.   He tries to get me to perform sex acts I
     dislike _____.

X.   He is the kind of man I would choose as
     an ideal father _____.

Y.   His friends respect me _____.

Z.   My family and friends like and respect
     him _____.

Write a paragraph describing what you learned
from this exercise — about yourself . . . your partner . . . your relationship.

_____

_____

_____

_____

_____

3)   Family of Origin

Our childhood histories affect how we relate to
significant others as adults. Each of us plays a role
in dysfunctional families. Discuss the role you
played in your family of origin, using the following
as guidelines:

A.   Rescuer

B. Problem child

C. Persecutor

D. Clown

E. Loner

F. Sickly child

Do you continue to play this role in adult relationships? What is the pay-off?

_____

_____

_____

_____

How does the role affect your relationship with your partner? Children? Friends? Parents?

_____

_____

_____

_____

Identify five times you reacted/acted as a victim as a child (at home, school). As an adult (at home, work). Are there similarities? Differences?

_____

_____

_____

_____

_____

4)   Core Beliefs and Patterns

     A.   What positive or negative messages did
          you get as a child about love, sex, mar-
          riage, men, women?

     _____

     _____

     _____

     B.   Do you see these scripts affecting your
          life today? How?

     _____

     _____

     _____

5)   Leaving an Abusive Relationship

     Victims often feel stuck and ambivalent about
     whether or not to remain with an abuser. List

the reasons why you should stay. List the reasons why you should leave. What conclusions can you draw from your writings? How would you feel if you left? Stayed?

_____

_____

_____

_____

_____

Think about degrees of abuse along the following continuum:

scapegoating	slapping	hitting	using weapons
criticizing ⇨	yelling ⇨	pushing ⇨	causing major
belittling	pushing	kicking	physical injury
		(resulting in	
		minor injury)	

Where does your relationship lie on the continuum? At what point has the line been crossed? At what point do you leave?

_____

_____

_____

6)   Maturity and Impulse Control

We all have ego states. Our adult (ego) medi-
ates with reality; our child feels; and our parent
evaluates and criticizes. For example, Mary
wants to "play hookie" from work. Her child
part tells her that she should go on a shopping
spree. Her parent part tells her that she should
not spend any money. Her adult part tells her
that she needs time off from work, deserves to
spend a certain amount of money, and should
ask her boss for a personal day of leave. Discuss one instance of how your adult, child, and
parent parts operated in your relationship with
your significant other.

7)   Control by the Victim

Abusers have power and control needs. Victims sometimes exercise power and control more
subtly, but in equally damaging ways, through inciting anger in perpetrators. Discuss how you exer-
cised control in your relationship with your
significant other. Use the following guidelines:

•   Through weakness

_____

_____

•   Through manipulation

_____

- Through moods (pouting, withdrawal)

_____

_____

- Using sex

_____

_____

- Using guilt

_____

_____

- Using (inciting) jealousy

_____

_____

- Using paybacks and expressing anger indirectly

_____

_____

8)   Charting Your Relationship

Too often, women describe their relationships with their significant others in terms of their feelings only. Thoughts, beliefs, judgments, and assessments are also important. Using the following statements, describe different ways you can view your relationship:

A. My feelings about the relationship physically (sexually)

_____

emotionally/psychologically

_____

intellectually

_____

behaviorally

_____

B. My beliefs about the relationship physically (sexually)

_____

_____

emotionally/psychologically

_____

_____

intellectually

_____

_____

behaviorally

_____

_____

C. My thoughts about the relationship physi-
    cally (sexually)

_____

_____

emotionally/psychologically

_____

_____

intellectually

_____

_____

behaviorally

For example, you may feel insecure sexually; unsatisfied emotionally; equal intellectually; and unhappy behaviorally while your beliefs and thoughts about the relationship may be quite different. Considering all aspects of the relationship helps you to make a more complete assessment in order to decide whether you should stay or leave.

9) Examining Abuse

Abuse is not static. It ebbs and flows in frequency and intensity (although over time there tends to be an escalation) and results in differing reactions among victims. Examine the abuse you have experienced in terms of:

- the pay-offs you derive

- the price you pay

- the effect on your self-esteem

- the emotions you experience

10) Emotional Expression

One of the by-products of abusive relationships is the dyscontrol of feelings for both the victim and perpetrator. Discuss how you han-

dle your emotions, particularly anger, using the
following questions as guidelines:

- Are you aware of your anger?

- Do you block, suppress, repress anger?

- Do you express anger appropriately (verbally and assertively)?

- Do you sublimate and channel anger
  through activities such as sports?

- Do you express anger passively or passive-
  aggressively?

- Do you internalize anger (with depression,
  chemicals, self-destructive acts)?

- Do you externalize acts (with violent behaviors, criminal acts)?

- Do you express anger through paybacks?

- Are you reactive or proactive with anger?

- Do you somaticize anger (through psychosomatic illnesses)?

- Do you deny, minimize, or rationalize anger?

- Do you displace anger onto others?

- Do you project anger, attributing the feelings to someone else?

11) Fantasies

Victims fantasize, daydream, and rationalize the faults of their abusers in order to justify the fact that they choose to stay in their relationships. They ruminate about their partners' potentials and abilities to change.

- How does your body feel when you deny reality?

- Do you feel emotionally anxious or upset?

- Do you get irritable when a friend or family member questions aspects of your relationship?

Try thought-stopping when you begin to fantasize. Try to reframe your fantasies. For example, instead of thinking, "He'll really love me once he becomes successful," reframe that thought: "If he doesn't love me now, he never will," and "I must deal with current reality, not his potential."

Try writing an unsent letter to your abuser dealing with the reality of your relationship and how it impacts your well-being.

APPENDIX D
Survey of Battered Women

■ Demographic Data

A. Age? _____

B. Current marital status? _____

C. Number of marriages? _____

D. Income and source? _____

E. Employed? _____ For how long? _____

F. Ethnic background (Caucasian, African-American, Latino, Native American, other)? _____

G. Children (number, ages, and current placement)? _____

H. Education

Elementary School? _____

High School? _____

College? _____

■ Childhood

A. During childhood, were you physically abused? _____ What occurred (beaten, spanked, shoved, hit)? _____

How often? _____ At what ages? _____

By whom? _____

B. Were you sexually abused during childhood? _____ What occurred (touched, fondled, raped)? _____

How often? _____ At what ages? _____

By whom? _____

■ Adulthood

A. Have you been raped (forced sex without consent)? _____ At what age(s)? _____ By whom?

_____

B. Have you abused/do you currently abuse alcohol? _____

Drugs? _____ Drugs and alcohol? _____

For how long? _____ Are you in recovery? _____

If so, for how long? _____

C.   Have you been physically abused by your partners? _____

By how many partners? _____ Frequently? _____

What acts of physical abuse were involved (hitting, shoving, spanking, punching, slapping, kicking)? _____

D.   What messages did you give yourself about the abuse? _____ About leaving? _____
About staying? _____ About the abuser? _____

Informal Survey Results

The survey was administered in 1996 to 25 women, all Caucasian, ages 19 to 51, with histories of battering, who were seen at a licensed behavioral health agency in the metropolitan Phoenix area.

Results

1)   Demographically, nine of the women were married at the time of the survey (four to their original batterers); three were single; 11 had been divorced; one, widowed; one, separated. Eleven of the women had been married previously to abusers.

Twenty of the women were from the lower socioeconomic classes in terms of education and finances. Five were in, or had completed, college.

Three of the women had experienced periods of homelessness. One was receiving disability for mental problems and four were receiving disability along with Aid to Families with Dependent Children (AFDC).

Twelve of the women were receiving AFDC and 12 were working, mostly part-time and without the knowledge of the state.

2)   Twenty-four of the 25 women were beaten, spanked, or hit daily or two or more times per week as children (from ages three to 16). The women were physically abused in birth, adoptive, and foster homes by parents, parent figures, and older brothers. Ten of the 24 women identified their mothers as abusers.

3)   Twenty of the 25 women were sexually molested by male relatives/caretakers from ages four to 15 with offenses frequent and ranging in intensity from fondling to rape. Sixteen identified more than one perpetrator.

4)   All 25 women said that they had been raped as adults, with rape defined as forced sex without consent. Dates and partners were the identified perpetrators.

5) Twenty-two of the 25 women had histories of chemical abuse (11 abused alcohol; four abused drugs; seven abused both drugs and alcohol). Abuse was long-term, since adolescence, with four in recovery since leaving their abusers.

6) All 25 of the women were physically abused by partners, with abuse defined as hitting, punching, slapping, kicking, shoving, and choking. Nineteen of the 25 had multiple perpetrators.

7) All 25 of the women remained with their abusers for a year or longer, with five leaving and returning several times. Only three sought help in the form of therapy with 11 claiming they did not seek counseling because their partners refused to accompany them.

8) The main reasons for remaining in abusive relationships were:

   - "He needs help . . ."
   - "He'll change . . ."
   - "The kids needed a father . . ."
   - "I had nowhere to go . . ."
   - "It wasn't so bad . . ."
   - "I had no mother."

   The main reasons for leaving were:

- "I'd finally had it . . . "
- "I thought he'd kill me."

9) Of the women who left, 12 did so by choice. Half of the women who left had options in terms of employment and family support. Five of the women were forced to leave with protective services threatening to remove the children or the arrest of the perpetrators. Seven of the women chose to remain in the relationships.

Discussions

This informal survey yielded some interesting results:*

1) Almost all of the women with histories of childhood physical and sexual abuse with a noteworthy number alleging physical abuse by their mothers. This finding is of particular interest since the roots of addictive and co-dependent relationships appear to relate to disrupted attachment issues during infancy.

2) Almost one-to-one relationship between battery and forced sex in domestic violence situations which corroborates the theory that rape is eroticized rage predicated on power and control needs.

---

*The prevalence of women in the sample from lower socioeconomic classes may be a function of where the survey was conducted, e.g., in a state-funded behavioral health agency.

3) Almost one-to-one relationship between battery and victim chemical abuse. Abused women anesthetize their feelings and self-medicate in order to cope with reality.

4) The reasons for remaining with abusive partners bearing no relationship to subsequent departures or decisions to stay with partners. Both those women who stayed, and those who stayed and finally left, referred to being needed, loving their abusers, and so forth. It appears that the women who left did so suddenly, having reached a saturation level with ongoing abuse or fearing that the abuse would escalate into life-or-death situations. The issue with abused women relates to the underlying dynamics that perpetuate the relationship. These dynamics are similar whether the women leave or stay.

5) None of the women voluntarily left for the sake of the children, which corroborates theories of addiction, co-dependence, and personality traits such as narcissism.

6) The high level of dysfunction of these victims with many of them receiving AFDC and disability, and several of them having experienced homelessness.

Annotated Reading List

Bloomfield, H.M. *Making Peace with Your Parents.* N.Y.: Ballantine Books, 1985.

📖 Insights and exercises on healing unresolved issues with parents; includes resentment, forgiveness, anger, love, and sexual messages; discusses types of parents, including martyrs and dictators.

Bilodeau, L. *The Anger Workbook.* Center City, Minn.: Hazelden, 1994.

📖 Attitudes and perspective on anger; includes exercises and information on how to alter expression and experience of anger.

Blumfeld, L. (Ed.). *The Big Book of Relaxation: Simple Techniques to Control the Excess Stress in your Life.* N.Y.: The Relaxation Co., 1994.

📖 Exercises on meditation, yoga, aromatherapy, music, breath, voice, and visualization; explains stress cycle; includes numerous exercises.

Engel, B. *The Emotionally Abused Woman: Overcoming Destructive Patterns and Reclaiming Yourself.* N.Y.: Fawcett Columbine, 1990.

📖 Recovery process for emotionally abused women; includes patterns of abuse; resolving unfinished issues; healing; breaking the cycle of abuse; parental scripts; confrontation of abusers; and decisions about leaving or staying in abusive relationships.

Frankel, L.P. *Women, Anger and Dependency: Strategies for Empowerment.* Deerfield Beach, FL: Health Communications, Inc., 1992.

📖 Explanation of anger; anger turned inward; PMS; includes exercises for self-awareness and change.

Grant, W. *Are You in Control? A Handbook for Those Who Want to be in Control of Their Lives.* Rockport, MA: Element Books, Inc., 1996.

📖 Confidence building; development of motivation, relaxation, relationships; includes exercises.

Halpern, H.M. *How to Break Your Addiction to a Person.* N.Y.: Bantam Books, 1983.

📖 Exploration of relationship between attachment hunger and addiction; provides strategies, techniques and exercises to break addictive patterns.

Kreisman, J.J. and Straus, H. *I Hate You. Don't Leave Me: Understanding the Borderline Personality.* N.Y.: Akron, 1989.

📖 Characteristics of borderline personalities; includes advice on management, communication, coping strategies, and medication.

Leider, R.J. *Life Skills: Taking Charge of Personal and Professional Growth.* San Diego, CA: Pfeiffer & Co., 1994.

📖 Goals, decision-making, evaluation of life skills, values clarification, and personal assessments

Macpherson, M.C. *The Psychology of Abuse.* Saratoga, CA: R & E Publishers, 1984.

📖 Description of characteristics of severly abused individuals; links traits with interruptions in normal developmental stages and emergence of sociopathic personalities.

Robertson, R. *Confessions of an Abusive Husband: A How-To Book for "Abuse-Free" Living for Everyone.* Lake Oswego, OR: Heritage Park Publishing, Co., 1992.

📖 Cycle of abuse, traits of abusers, 12-step recovery process, and anger management.

Sonkin, D.J. and M. Durphy. *Learning to Live Without Violence: A Handbook for Men.* San Francisco, CA: Volcano Press, 1985.

📖 Insights on domestic violence for victims and perpetrators; includes exercises on anger control, stress, chemical abuse, communication, and feelings; provides log forms and journaling instructions.

References

Beattie, M. *Co-Dependent No More.* Center City. Minn.: Hazelden, 1987.

Berkowitz, L. "The Goals of Aggression." In (Eds.) D. Finkelhor, R. J. Gelles, G. T. Hotaling, and M. A. Straus. *The Dark Side of Families: Current Family Violence Research.* Beverly Hills, CA: Sage, 1983.

Becker, R.A. *Addicted to Misery: The Other Side of Co-Dependency.* Deerfield Beach, FL: Health Communications, Inc., 1989.

Black, C. *It Will Never Happen to Me.* Denver, CO: Medical Administration, 1982.

Browne, A. *When Battered Women Kill.* N.Y.: The Free Press, 1987.

Cobbs, C. "Sports: A Culture of Denial," *The Arizona Republic,* March 11, 1996.

Coleman, K.H., M. L. Weinman, and B. P. Hsi. "Factors Affecting Conjugal Violence," *Journal of Psychology,* 105, 1980, 197-202.

Davidson, M.T. *Conjugal Crime: Understanding and Changing the Wife-Beating Pattern.* N.Y.: Hawthorn Books, Inc., 1978.

Dowling, C. *The Cinderella Complex: Women's Hidden Fear of Independence.* N.Y.: Pocket Books, 1981.

Dutton, D.G. *The Batterer: A Psychological Profile.* N.Y.: Basic Books, 1995.

Engel, B. *The Emotionally Abused Woman: Overcoming Destructive Patterns and Reclaiming Yourself.* N.Y.: Fawcett Columbine, 1990.

Fagan, J.A., D. K. Stewart, and K. V. Hanson. "Violent Men or Violent Husbands?" In (Eds.) D. Finkelhor, R. J. Gelles, G. T. Hotaling, and M. A. Straus. *The Dark Side of Families: Current Family Violence Research.* Beverly Hills, CA: Sage, 1983.

Forward, S. *Men Who Hate Women and the Women Who Love Them.* N.Y.: Bantam Books, 1986.

Gelles, R.J. and Straus, M.A. *Intimate Violence.* N.Y.: Simon and Schuster, 1988.

Gelles, R.J. *The Violent Home.* Newbury Park, CA: Sage Publications, Inc., 1987.

Halpern, H. *How to Break Your Addiction to a Person.* N.Y.: Bantam, 1983.

Halpern, H. *Cutting Loose: An Adult Guide to Coming to Terms with Your Parents.* N.Y.: Simon and Schuster, 1977.

Hare, R.D. *Without Conscience: The Disturbing World of the Psychopath Among Us.* N.Y.: Pocket Books, 1993.

James, B. *Handbook for Treatment of Attachment Trauma Problems in Children.* N.Y.: Lexington Books, 1994.

Launius, M.H. and C.V. Lindquist. "Learned Helplessness, External Locus of Control and Passivity in Battered Women," *Journal of Interpersonal Violence,* Vol. 3, no. 3, (September 1988): 307-19.

Jones, A. *Next Time She'll Be Dead: Battering and How to Stop It.* Boston: Beacon, 1994.

Miller, D.M. *Re-Union: Healing our Victim and Offender Patterns.* Chandler, AZ: Serenity Publications, 1993.

Miller, J. *Addictive Relationships: Reclaiming Your Boundaries.* Deerfield Beach, FL: Health Communications, Inc., 1989.

Norwood, R. *Women Who Love Too Much.* Los Angeles: Jeremy P. Tarcher, 1985.

Kiley, D. *The Wendy Dilemma.* N.Y.: Arbor House Publishers, 1984.

Phelps, J.K. and A.E. Nourse. *The Hidden Addictions and How to Get Free.* Boston: Little Brown, 1986.

Peabody, S. *Addiction to Love: Overcoming Obsession and Dependency in Relationships.* Berkeley, CA: Ten Speed Press, 1989.

Robertson, R. *Confessions of an Abusive Husband: A "How-To" Book for Abuse-Free Living for Everyone.* Lake Oswego, OR: Heritage Park Publishing Co., 1992.

Rubin, J. *The Angry Book.* N.Y.: MacMillan, 1970.

Russell, D.E.H., and N. Van de Ven. (Eds.) *Crimes Against Women: Proceedings of the International Tribunal.* East Palo Alto, CA: Frog-in-the-Well, 1984.

Silverman, L.H., F.M. La Chann, and R.H. Millich. *The Search for Oneness.* N.Y.: International Universities Press, 1982.

Walker, L.E. *Terrifying Love: Why Women Kill and How Society Responds.* N.Y.: Harper Perennial, 1990.

Walker, L. *The Battered Woman.* N.Y.: Harper & Row, 1979.

Wegscheider, S. *Another Chance: Hope and Health for the Alcoholic Family.* Palo Alto: Science and Behavior Books, 1981.

Woititz, J.G. *Adult Children of Alcoholics.* Hollywood, FL: Health Communications, 1983.